Jessie,
This is a book
I give to only very
special people. You
being the finest example
of one.

Jerry

IN MAINE

IN MAINE

"Of all the winds that blow,
I like the northwest best...."

by John N. Cole

EDITOR OF *MAINE TIMES*

WITH PHOTOGRAPHS BY STEPHEN BROWN NICHOLS

A Harpswell Press Book
E. P. Dutton & Co., Inc.   /   New York   /   1974

FOREWORD

Because he runs a crisp, informative, outspoken weekly, John Cole is probably most widely known as a good, somewhat flammable newspaperman. This is true, of course, and especially so because of the perceptive and unambiguous positions he and Maine Times take on issues of importance in the region. But the description, however complimentary, is not really adequate, for John Cole is more than that. He is also a fine writer unafraid to express his deep personal feelings, even his considerable tenderness. It is this quality of simple candor, I think, that truly distinguishes him and gives "John's Column" a special stature wherever readers feel themselves natural companions of the land, of the wind, of the sea. In the good tradition of earlier essayists, John Cole dares to seek and hail discoveries in his own interior landscape. Thus he can stir others to strong action or to surprising personal findings. Many of the pieces in this book read like walkers' maps to forgotten sites of the self.

John's earlier, pre-Maine life, what little I knew of it, was in some ways a preparation for his passionate affair with Maine. We were boys together, sort of. That is, we rode some of the same waves back to a lovely Long Island beach, took bicycle pursuit of the same tanned, long-legged girls, poured the same forbidden Scotch whiskey down gagging gullets at dress-up winter parties in New York City. We were friends although we didn't see a whole lot of each other, and I remember being jealous of John because he could talk authoritatively about subjects like shotguns and rods and crabbing. I also admired his nerve for doing things we weren't supposed to do. According to parental rankings of the period, his father was supposed to be even stricter than my own, and I can recall watching John pedal stoically off home into the darkness fifteen minutes after his curfew hour had passed with the sense that he was headed for unspeakable reprisals.

As I remember, John was always more involved than most kids with the natural world he shared. He really studied the life of a big pond not far from his place and spent hours just fooling around the little gut that connected the pond with the sea. The story he tells in one of these columns about sneaking away from a summer dance is characteristically adventurous. It gives me both delight and envy to read how he found the fishermen that night and then helped them haul their full net up on the beach. I can guess where I was at the time — trapped back there at the party with some miserable adult on his fourth martini who was bullying me to remember that I had to dance with every girl at my table.

"All my worst memories are man-made," John writes here, and the statement makes me not sorry I don't know all that it's taken to make him the man and writer he's come to be. Anyhow, it's obvious that the time he spent as a commercial fisherman off Long Island's Montauk was terribly important to him, much more so than the tinkling life he absconded from in New York where he was at one time legman for an influential evening paper columnist. Anyone the slightest bit familiar with John Cole or his columns knows that he is a very tidal person, much more susceptible to pulls from the moon than to any artificial excitements the man-made city can offer. Silence is itself a kind of orchestration for him, and he marks the seasons as carefully as if someone long ago had made him promise to do it.

Thus Maine offers a marvelous lodging place for many of John Cole's feelings about life and about himself. And he gives a lot back. He finds hope in the worst winters that better ones are coming. "How long would a winter be without a chickadee," he writes, and his ability to draw this pure kind of comfort gives time a seamless quality in the best of his pieces. He rides time like a wave or the northwest wind he loves — back to his childhood, then through his life and manhood to his own children and their growing joy in life. John Cole strikes me as the kind of man who will take a close but easy interest in his age, when he gets old, and not worry much about what might happen next. Why should he worry? Things have always worked out pretty well for him. He used to be a striped bass, John tells us.

Loudon Wainwright

CONTENTS

for my brown-eyed friend

INTRODUCTORY

Well, it's March—an anniversary month for me. The month my father was born, and died; the month my son was born; the month of the vernal equinox; and the month I first set foot in Maine.

With that cast of characters, March is assured of a starring role in my memories for the rest of my years. In a way, that's good, because March in Maine offers little else but time—a gray stretch of it between the end of winter and hope for spring. March is no season; or it is a season unto itself, mixing winter, spring and parts of autumn as its whims decide, independent of the calendar and weather charts.

March had opted for 100 percent winter at the moment I chose to embark in Maine. That was at 3 a.m. on a mid-March pre-dawn precisely twelve years ago. I came to Kennebunk from Dayton, Ohio, with several jolting interruptions along the way. The first was on a turnpike near Buffalo. It had been snowing hard there—a wet, heavy snow hurled from the Great Lakes. I was driving a blown Oldsmobile convertible—a racy looking but totally impractical car which had, at one time, belonged to my sister in her years of flaming youth and monetary success as a New York designer. In a now unremembered change of life styles, she had abandoned her car, moved away and left the machine on blocks for two years in the garage where I found it when I was Dayton-bound and needed wheels.

The old Olds survived two years in Ohio, but it didn't last the return trip. Those days on blocks had rusted too many oil lines and corroded too much of the engine's energy. Pushing through the soft snow of Buffalo, the Olds crunched two pistons and slowed to a mortally wounded, stuttering crawl. I nursed it off the turnpike, and into one of the first Buffalo garages I could find. I was in a bit of a bind. I had about $20 to get me the rest of the way to Maine, and that was the extent of my cash reserves. My family was in Dayton, and our furniture was being sold at ridiculous prices to finance their move.

I telephoned the only person I knew in Buffalo, a college class-mate. I was told he was off playing polo in Del Ray, Florida—a bit of information which only served to give another shake to the coals of bitterness already burning in my gut. The garage mechanic informed me the Olds needed a new engine. At least I was rational enough to be able to laugh at that diagnosis. In the end, I traded him a bottle of going-away-gift fine whiskey (which a Daytonian had laid on me as I left) for about 40 gallons of waste oil drained from oil-change crankcases as I hung around. I put the oil in five and ten-gallon drums that dripped over the snappy red leather seats and drove the wheezing Olds another couple of hundred miles, keeping my speed around 30 mph and stopping every 20 miles or so to fill the spewing engine with more of the black crankcase waste. It was, to say the least, an ignominious journey for a man on his way to be a Maine editor.

It became even more shattering, and quite rapidly, too. Ah, but that's another long and horrendous story. At its conclusion, I had to abandon the Olds at an Albany service station and struggle on to Maine on the bus—even as carless folk are still struggling today, twelve years later.

It was the last bus out of Boston that I got, and it was snowing there when we left. When we crossed the New Hampshire-Massa-chusetts border, we were greeted with a full blown blizzard.

By the time we got to Kennebunk there was about six inches of new snow howling through the windy night, and more than a foot already on the ground—a leftover from the storm that had crippled the Olds in Buffalo. The bus stopped on Kennebunk's Main Street, I got off, shouldered my duffle bag, watched the bus leave and began walking through the dark blizzard down a street I had never walked toward a house I had never seen. My directions for getting there were on a letter in my pocket, and it was too dark to read. The snow drifts reached my knees, the wind was bitter cold and I thought to myself that I had come all this way to be frozen into a snow bank and found there the next day, an anony-mous vagrant, casually abandoned and tossed to extinction.

But the town plow came by, followed by the town police cruiser driven by Kennebunk patrolman Frank Stevens (now Chief) and he stopped and gave me a ride to where I wanted to go. The cruiser got stuck, I had to push it out; my host was too sound asleep to answer the storm-muffled knocks on his locked door and Frank drove me back to the Kennebunk Inn where I got a few hours of rest before reporting for work at my new newspaper job on my first day in Maine.

A few days later, Spring arrived, and so did the new life I am still living.

Of my four-plus decades, only the Sixties saw me living the entire span in the same area and working at the same job for ten years. Before the Sixties came along to settle me down, I hadn't lived in any one place for more than three years, and the number of different jobs I had held would average out to more than two a year. But it was 1960 when I moved to Brunswick (where I still am) to become editor of a weekly newspaper (which I still am, although it's not the same newspaper).

Because of the relative continuity of my life over the past ten years, I can look back and see the Sixties more clearly than I've seen any of my other three decades on this earth. Don't, for example, ask me to make any order out of how I spent the Fifties; they don't hold together for me at all. But I can recall distinctly arriving in Brunswick in the summer of 1960 with pro-Stevenson bumper stickers on my car. And I can still see the television footage of that year's national Democratic convention which kept me up too late for a fellow who was starting a new job as editor of the weekly *Brunswick Record*.

We answered the phones late election night at the *Record* office. I wept the only election tears of my life at the news that Frank Coffin had been defeated by Maine Governor John Reed; but the next day I was cheered at the long delayed results of the national squeaker that put John F. Kennedy in the White House.

Life went well for me as editor of the *Brunswick Record*. The newspaper's circulation grew; some recognition from my fellow professionals began to drift my way. In the early days of the Sixties I realized for the first time the comfort of knowing there was something on the earth I could do with some competence. John Kennedy was inaugurated President in the same January snowstorm that trapped me in Boston at my first meeting with regional newspapermen. I was watching a hotel television set when Robert Frost read his poem, Cardinal Cushing droned his prayer and smoke began to drift from under the Inaugural lectern.

Then came the Cuban crisis, the great civil rights march on Washington on August of '63, the 99th and the 101st Legislatures in Maine and the first major river classification law that was intended to clean up the Kennebec. I had moved from Bowdoinham to Brunswick by then. Walt Disney had the children's favorite hour on television. Ingmar Bergman and Marilyn Monroe were making the most talked about films.

I was 600 miles out in the North Atlantic on a 147-foot government exploratory fishing vessel—the Delaware—when the ship got the radio message that gray November day in '63 that John Kennedy had been shot dead in Dallas. In that bleak, wild and wintry world of open water, the news seemed even more unreal to me than it must have to most Americans. It took days for reality to make its impact.

During 1964 and on into '65, *Record* columnist David Graham began to write more and more about a little publicized war in Vietnam. As I read David's words, I also began to write in opposition to the land war that I considered both immoral and impractical. Stanley Tupper, Kenneth Curtis and Lyndon Johnson were elected, and once again we kept late hours at the *Record* to answer election night telephones. By then, I was an experienced enough editor not to be exhausted by the event.

My children were beginning junior high school. They were becoming people, taking on the characters and interests that make them individuals. Both they and myself were listening to a new singing group, The Beatles, whose long hair was just beginning to set a youthful fashion that has become a *cause celebre*. Watts burned, Newark burned, Vietnamese civilians burned. Malcolm X was shot; Cassius Clay belted Sonny Liston in Lewiston. I wrote about that for the *Brunswick Record* in its last year as a weekly. In 1967, Peter Cox and myself became co-editors of Maine's newest daily, the *Bath-Brunswick Times Record*, and I had to work the new, more frantic pace of a daily.

I was in New York City, staying in a hotel just across 65th Street from the place where I had lived as a child, on my first vacation from the *Times-Record* in April of '68 when Walter Cronkite ended his evening news broadcast with the report of Martin Luther King's murder. We listened to the sirens through the night, and I wept, for myself, the man and the nation. I wept again at 5:30 on a June morning two months later when I turned on the radio as I began shaving and grooming for my daughter's graduation from junior high school, and the radio voice told me Robert Kennedy had been shot.

A few months later, Peter and I produced the first copy of the *Maine Times*. We are still at it. The Beatles, the drugs and the beautiful young are still with us, but their leaders have been murdered. *Maine Times* looks as if it will be here in 1979. I pray that then I will not have memories as violent as those that so overshadow my Sixties.

Every person should have one good year. I can say that because I know that 1969 was a good year for me, and I have it now to look back on, to roll around in my memory circuits the way a small boy savors a bit of hard candy as he slides its sweetness from one side of his taste buds to the other.

It wasn't the year I won the Sweepstakes, or anything like that— no single momentous event exploded in my life, marking a sudden change from unhappy to happy, poor to rich, or sick to healthy. Instead, 1969 was a fine collection of contentments—moments following moments of peace, accomplishment, beauty, wildness, excitement and smiles.

I had *Maine Times*, of course, moving through its first full calendar year. There is nothing quite like a new project to keep a man occupied; something about the very newness makes more time demands than would the same job if it became routine.

Watching *Maine Times* survive was the key to the goodness of my 1969. It was the publication's most critical year—the time when it could have been too starved for sustenance to grow, or too rejected by its public to endure. But 1969 brought enough sustenance, and the public brought an acceptance full enough to surpass even my own, unspoken dreams.

Maine Times, in short, became a success in 1969, and sharing that success put warmth in each of my months. But it was more than occupational good fortune that kept the year aglow. The weather, in my memory, worked to make '69 a good year for living in Maine country. Last winter was as snowy as any in my lifetime; I can still see the towering snowbanks that rose like cliffs at the roadside, so high they hid behind them scores of houses that lined the road-edge. As I drove, every now and then I could see a chimney or a rooftop, but most often I saw smoke rising to mark a home the snow had made invisible.

All that snow let me ski long enough to persuade myself that I had improved. On one of the last weekends in April, as I was spring skiing on the kind of spring snow they write about in magazines, I began to make turns I had thought impossible for me. That was my last day on skis for the year; and that, too, is as it should be. (I am seriously considering never skiing again.)

We had a rich spring at our house. From Memorial Day on through the summer, every flower and blossom on the place seemed to bloom more brightly than ever; and through the summer there were boys enough to keep the lawn mowed without me. That was good, because I was fishing much of the time. I found just enough stripers last summer to keep us all in fresh fish; and enough large ones to break my lines and twist my lures. With fishing like that, the two bluefish I hooked in Middle Bay were a flashing dividend of joy declared by the sea gods just for me.

There were crystal summer days at the beach, summer twilights on the water, and one summer midnight under a full moon on a bay so full of feeding stripers that fish sounds actually made the darkness noisy. Marsh and I might have caught some of those fish later in September's last days when we traveled to Montauk and the Can-Am races at Bridgehampton. We had a good vacation, a fine visit, and got right next to the racing machines, their drivers and the drivers' racy ladies.

No one in the family was sick during the year. No suitcases blew off the top of the car; no trips had to be cancelled, confused or contrived. The sump pump never failed; the septic tank didn't back up; no fenders were dented even though the boys had their driving licenses for the first time. It was my first full year as a non-smoker, and I managed to make it with hardly a tremor of temptation, although I quivered with righteous pride every time someone mentioned how impossible it had been for them to give up the weed.

1969 was also the year I began to discover Maine. As part of my occupation, I traveled to many Maine towns I had never visited before, and I met hundreds of Maine people I never could have met any other way. My discoveries were a delight; as I have written here during this past good year, Maine's beauty is draped like a fine cape across the entire body of the state, and Maine people are hospitable no matter where they're found. I don't yet truly know even a small part of Maine; but I do know that each of my Maine discoveries has been a happy event.

A year like 1969—365 days of relative serendipity and good fortune—can do a great deal for a fellow. It gives his entire life a better image, makes him forget many bad times. It also gives me a bit of anxiety about 1970; how could it possibly be as good, especially when I'm starting it with the first cold I've had in a year.

THE SEASONS

The summer change has come. No matter how warm the days between now and October, the full softness of summer will never return — not until another year. Sometimes the weather turn hesitates until late August; it seldom arrives as early as it did this season. But there is no mistaking its presence.

The summer change is never a lightning bolt or a killing frost — nothing as dramatic or noticeable as that. It is instead the faltering entrance of a feeling, something in the air, a new composition of atmospheric molecules that makes itself known within a man's soul before it shows up on the weather charts or in the almanacs. Perhaps you have never noticed it; perhaps I am making it up, imagining something that doesn't exist, but if I am, I have been imagining the same phenomena for all of my rememberable life.

It came a bit more than a week ago. I had stepped outdoors through the new "side door" we had punched through where the dining room window used to be. I walked across the lawn to look at a lilac shoot I had been given by a friend who has the loveliest lilacs in Maine. On my way I passed the two ancient apple trees that gnarl themselves over the tiny flower garden, and I noticed how heavy the apples hung from the brittle branches. Hadn't it been just a few days before that the same branches were flattered to new beauty by a million bursting blossoms?

But it was not the apples that brought the summer change to my attention, although my awareness of their limb-bending weight might have tuned me in more precisely to the message I was about to receive. I walked across the lawn, found the infant lilac thriving and turned to go back to the house. As I walked over the rain-hungry grass, I felt the coolness of the breeze on my cheek. I understood immediately what it was saying, and when I got back to the doorway I knew that I had not misunderstood. For until that day, the sheltered air that sits so still by our side door had been a haven for flying mites — mini-squadrons of winged midgets so small that they are forever invisible until they sink their micro-stingers into an earlobe or a forearm.

Their raids began instantaneously whenever we went out that door. Often before I could even don my poise for some unexpected guest, I would find myself under attack by my invisible, but lethal foes. The mites loved it there in that sun-warmed, wind-sheltered, safe place; but on that evening last week they had been routed by the summer change. Nothing I had been able to do (including un-told gallons of kerosene spray, or personal defenses based on L. L. Bean's "Woodsman's Friend" insect repellent) had been successful in shooting down the artful dodgers. But the summer change had done them in, and when I put their absence together with the preponderance of apples and the cool breeze on my cheek, I knew that at that moment I had been witness to a phenomenon.

I recognized it readily. Of each of the weather turns that comes each year, I welcome this one most, even more that the winter change that comes in early February when a spring wind moves wetly over the snow.

Perhaps because this summer has seemed to go so quickly, perhaps because the summer change came so early, I have remembered the moment with such clarity. Yet there are other reasons for marking it in memory. For with the summer change comes a rush of scenes from the past, a tumbling of memories from child-hood through the scores of times the new autumn wind has trans-formed the meaning of my days. For in New England, the seasons work true wonders with the minds of men; and if you ignore the impact of the seasons here, you can make an important mistake. It is the seasons that bring vitality.

The size of your error was there that evening. Nothing around here will be quite the same until next June. Men will move with more energy, greater purpose, larger and more splendid dreams. This is what happens with the summer change; the autumn air that is here now is charged with some special ozonal elixir that lifts men from their normal monotony, and gives them some power source drawn from ancient migratory instincts. It propels them into a renewal of purpose and an explosion of creativity.

If you don't believe me, flip back through the file cards of your memory, and see if the boldest type isn't printed on those filed under "Fall."

Of all the winds that blow, I like the northwest best. It is rare as a summer wind along this upper corner of the Atlantic coast, but in late August the first nor'westers return, bringing clarity, excitement and an energy that has been missing from the prevailing southerly breezes that so damply dominate New England Junes and Julys.

In this part of the world, the northwest wind wings in behind the ridges of high barometric pressure that move from west to east (at about 15 miles per hour, as I recall). You can tell when it's coming merely by listening to radio reports of weather conditions in Albany, Burlington and Buffalo. Or, more accurately, you can watch your barometer for the needle's eager upward surge toward "fair."

Best of all, you can stand in the meadow behind your home, as I stood in mine last week, and look to the western sky for the wind's arrival. When the highs move in, they most often are rushing on the heels of a low which tugs at them with an atmospheric vacuum. The lows often bring dampness, rain, clouds, humidity, drizzle and depression. As these visibles disappear, the signals of the northwest wind are flown on the western horizon.

Even though there may be solid, bulbous gray clouds draping the heavens overhead, in the far west the gloomy blanket begins to rip. Its edge pulls away from the rim of the land, exposing a sliver of pale blue. Once pulled away, the cloud curtain rises more quickly, its edge becoming more clearly defined until it stretches in a great arc that runs across the sky's zenith, leaving one half of the heavens gray, the other blue — as if the clouds were some sort of mechanical canopy that was being rolled back from the roof of a great dome that covers the world.

Generally all is still as the clouds roll back. Yet in the silence, it seems as if the sounds of rejoicing are everywhere. The sun is bright — brighter than ever because of the rain which has just washed the air and because the sun's new brilliance contrasts so with the vanishing darkness of the cloud curtain. (I have watched the weather change at night too; and then, as the cloud screen lifts, the hard bright stars appear as if they had just been set ablaze.)

It is out of this brilliant stillness that the northwest wind is born. The leaves rustle first, the meadow grass bends, the willow boughs swing, there is a sigh from the elm, and then, announced by the first cottony puff of a fair weather cloud in the west, like smoke from a cannon, the northwest wind arrives in a blustery rush, pushing up whitecaps on the bay, sweeping an ever increasing fleet of plump clouds through the sky, turning damp to dry, hot to cool, apathy to alacrity, depression to joy...making life everywhere better than it was before and reminding me every time of why it is important to know which way the wind blows.

I did not always know. As a boy in New York City I walked most often with my grandfather, and we walked together in the city in the fall and winter and spring. Our travels on foot often took us to the corner of 58th Street and Fifth Avenue, at the southeastern corner of Central Park, across from the Plaza, and bordering a large open square presided over by the gilded figure of some conquering general riding a golden horse far above the pigeons and people that swirled beneath the silent hooves. That corner at 58th and Fifth was "Windy Corner" in my grandfather's personal guidebook, and we would make a show of bracing ourselves for the wind that often swirled there, blowing away hats and hurling bits of city grit into the eyes of the unwary. I didn't know it then, but it was the northwest wind that made that place Windy Corner; and it was on the high days of good weather brought by the nor'-westers that my grandfather would take us walking.

As the years passed and I walked alone in the city, I never walked that corner without remembering. And I seldom walked without resenting the city grit that eroded the romance of my memories. It was on that corner that my environmental education was begun, that my weather consciousness was awakened, that I began to become aware of which way the wind blew.

My education was accelerated in another classroom: the pond in front of my grandfather's summer place, 120 miles from Windy Corner on a narrow finger of ground between the pond and the open Atlantic. On a late March Saturday I filled my day alone (my grandfather was busy at pre-season chores) with building a burlap sail for our old rowboat, rowing across the pond directly into the slapping whitecaps, raising the sail at the opposite shore and hissing home at the highest speed the ancient skiff had ever traveled. I was about eleven then, and I did that all day. It was the most exciting day of my life to that point. I did not know it then, but it had been brought to me by the northwest wind.

The chief reason for the day's continued importance is that when that weekend was over, I thought seriously about refusing to go back to the city. It took another twenty years for me to convert the thought to action, and it began with the northwest wind.

I am no longer sailing the same waters I did as a fisherman more than a decade ago, but much of the same exuberance I knew off Montauk is still part of my life. It is a welcoming of the days, an arms-wide greeting, an embrace of all the hours. And the hours that are most cherished are those that fly in on the wings of the northwest wind.

In Maine, the wind still moves as it has for eons. There are few cities to baffle it with their fingers of concrete and glass, few factories to soil it with smoke and sulphur, few engines to override it with noise or charge it with monoxide. Here I can live with the free wind as I lived with it off Montauk where all winds clean themselves in the sea.

In Maine, I have watched the wind being born, birthing in the western sky and then feathering the bay's silken surface with the first tentative touch of its young pinions. I have seen the nor' westers make a sea of our meadow, rolling the high grass in waves that break on the crest of our hill. And I have felt the same wind fill a sail with a hard slap that sets my boat a running.

It does the same to me. It dashes its fresh chill in my face, clears my head and sets my thoughts a running. Of the nor'west thoughts, the one that echoes loudest each September is the one about knowing....knowing which way the wind blows.

What has happened is that too many men decided they no longer needed to know. The decision came in a rush that had been building for tens of centuries when all men lived always with the wind. They knew the same wind that brought the fat ducks in the fall also brought its cutting edge in winter. They watched the wind dry their saved soil to dust and blow it to the sea; they witnessed the wind-made waves that sent their sailing ships ashore, crushing the souls within like so much chaff. For them the wind was more cruel than kind; certainly cruelty often came mixed with kindness.

Then, just a moment ago on the century clock, men learned how to build temples the wind could not torment, ships the wind could not sink, fields that could not be flayed. Because the wind was subjugated, it was also forgotten; or, if not forgotten, shelved, set aside, ignored to the point where most men arose in their temples and set forth on their days without knowing which way the wind blew, without caring, without looking, without seeing.

This ignorance of the wind might have been expected (after centuries of being awed by it), but it is not natural. Men can not live without knowing...knowing which way the wind blows, which way the rain falls, how the sea surges, the land lives and the forests die.

Yet there are multiple millions of men who don't know; men who live in cities, in windowless walls, who walk Windy Corner and notice nothing more than city grit — much more of it now than when I walked there as a child. How to tell them which way the wind is blowing; how to get them to know the nor'west experience; how to dash its fresh chill in their face, to set them to thinking, to set their boats to running — how to do that is one of the puzzles I ponder most when the northwest wind fills my Maine days.

Some of the answer, I decide, must be here in Maine. The other afternoon I counted seven sparrow hawks flying over the field, or perched beside it. The tiny falcons had been brought here on the wings of the northwest wind. It is the parent bird of the falcons, and they fly with it for all their fall migration to the south. They will stay in the field now until the northwest wind returns; then they will leave and a new band of hawks will be blown in. Along with them will come the plover, the geese, the teal, the curlew and the coot. They, and their wind, will enrich each of my autumn days until the wind locks away the bays behind a wall of ice.

Today is an autumn day, and as I watch the falcons fly under the wings of the northwest wind, I wish the same sight could be seen by the millions who have forgotten why the wind blows, or how, or where.

After seeing Maine in September, they may forget no more.

There are some good reasons why I can write about clams with affection and authority. Clams were my survival during my first winter as a commercial fisherman. That was an especially cold winter, and it came just a few months after I had abandoned my desk job in New York City to become a fisherman of the bay and ocean waters off the easternmost tip of Long Island (N.Y.). The golden autumn days were a joy, much as they are now. Few realities life can muster are capable of destroying the zest and richness of September and October in this northeast. It is a migratory season for all creatures, and the oceanic crossroads off Montauk Point teem with fish in such numbers that even a first-year novice can find sustenance catching blues and bass, or dredging scallops from the winey waters.

In my first year the autumn soared by on the wings of my own exhilaration at being free and fishing. The momentum of those days rolled me through November with scarcely a tremor, even though there was ice to break some mornings in the bottom of the dory. Then came December, the bleak dusk we stood freezing on the beach knowing the last fish had gone by. The boats and nets were stored away till spring, and many of my fishing friends went south; others sailed offshore on large trawlers; still others geared up for cod fishing; and a few readied for clamming. Because clamming was the simplest of the choices, because it required the lowest investment, and because I was constantly told that a "strong back and a weak mind" were the only prerequisites for succeeding as a clammer, I chose to clam.

It was, far beyond all else, the most agonizing work I have ever done. In those waters, we clammed for hard clams from small boats — craft that are called rowboats, punts, or flat-bottomed skiffs. Off Montauk, they are called sharpies — a name I always thought derived from the sharp bow that wedged out to the broad, flat stern in a slightly curved geometric triangle. There are two winter ways to clam from sharpies. One is to bull rake, which requires the clammer to stand in the sharpy bow and work a long handled, monstrously heavy curved steel basket of a 32-toothed bull rake into the mud 10 or 15 feet down, raking out the hard clams (quahogs) from their deep winter beds. Because I didn't know how to work the rake properly, or how to get it to work for me, I constantly broke the long, yellow pine handles. I would be back home at 10 a.m. with a peck of clams and two broken handles.

I had to abandon the bull rake and try tongs. Tonging for clams also requires standing at the gunwale of a sharpy; but for this system, the primary tool is the tongs, rather like old fashioned sugar tongs, with long wooden handles with basketed steel rakes on the ends. Instead of pinching a sugar cube, the clam tongs work down into a sandy bottom, opening and closing as the digger alternately parts and closes the long handles. Every now and then the groping rakes close on a clam, or two, and with a delicate lifting motion, the creature is pulled from his place, jostled into the basket, and hauled hand over hand in the closed tongs to the surface. I did it one clam at a time.

I found a small spot in Napeague Bay that had been abandoned by other clammers because the only clams left there were scattered, huge "chowder" quahogs — immense, heavy shelled creatures which brought less than $4.00-a-bushel on the New York market. But they were easy for me to find with the tongs, and the small bay was protected from the worst of the winter winds.

Even in the snow and sleet, I could and did clam at Napeague during that January and February. Every gray morning I would slide the old *Emma* (my sharpy, named after my grandmother, from whom it had been "borrowed") into the bay, anchor over the spot and tong out two bushels of big chowders. Mine was the only boat on the bay; I was the only person for miles. The tiny summer cottages around the bay's edge were closed; the wind tore across the snowy dunes and the briny ice that rimmed the empty shore. Only a few herring gulls kept me company, and the pain in my cold-numbed fingers often brought tears to my eyes.

But on Fridays, I had a respite. Because the New York prices were so low for my kind of quahogs, I would hold my clams in our garage. By Thursday I would have eight bushels or so, and on Thursday nights I would shuck them all and package the meats in one-quart containers. Then, on Friday, instead of going to the bay, I would sell my clams, door-to-door. I would keep selling until I was sold out, even if it meant I had to work after dark — not a good practice for a door-to-door salesman. When I was through, I'd have enough money to sustain my family. If it hadn't been for those clams, I would probably have gotten so discouraged that I might have given up my entire adventure and gone back to the city to find a job I didn't want in a place I didn't like.

26

That's why I have such an affection for clams and sympathy for clam diggers. Those quahogs got me through the first winter of fishing, and fishing changed me for always. It was almost April when I quit peddling. The sun was warm that Friday morning, and as I approached one back porch I surprised a dozing Chesapeake retriever who bit me hard just above the kneecap before I let him have it with a quart container. I knew there were no surly dogs along the beach where the bass were just starting their spring run, so I left my clams on that lawn and went to see Capt. Ted about a job with his seining crew.

There are moments in Maine's Septembers when time stops, suspended at the vortex of seasonal change like a woodchip motionless in a whirlpool's calm center. There was just such a moment last Wednesday evening. It came after the equinoctial violence of a nor'east gale, and before a freshening nor'west wind. In that timeless interim, at the eye of summer's end and autumn's beginning, came a cloudless and windless presence that took the sea and sky and land into another dimension without hours and minutes, manmade motion or mechanical stress.

There was movement, of course, but movement within a droplet of time suspended. The sun hung over the evening horizon, the air was so clear that it seemed not there, and the waters of the bay shone back at the sky with a luminosity glowing from some mysterious depth. Over all was that particular September serenity which everyone has felt, but few can describe. Yet it can be shared, and surely anyone who stepped outdoors last Wednesday remembers it well.

I was near the bay, had come to do a chore but abandoned it for the quality of the evening. As I looked out over the golden waters, great schools of striped bass moved into our part of the cove, gulls wheeled over them and I rowed the dory out to the middle of the fish. They are seen this way only in September. It is their massing before migration. Like the herring, the teal, the plover and the tern, the fish which have been moving separately through Maine's summer waters gather in September to move collectively to the south and the Chesapeake where they will winter over.

As the schools gather and grow, the bass feed mightily, packing in the energy for their trip, trying to store enough surplus to draw on during their single-minded surge to the south. This evening they drove the spattering shining schools of herring into still shoal waters, where I drifted amongst them in my dory, turning ever-so-slowly in the windless timeless tide.

I was alone on the entire bay, and my times past rushed to fill the temporal bell jar. Like the fish surging to the surface in a sudden silver splash, the people of my past who should have been there to share the evening surged to the surface of my ken. These were the "acres of bass" that Jim had said so many times we would someday find; Roddy's wraith rested on the stern thwart, studying the wheeling gulls; Wyman Aldrich who had taken me fishing when he was old and I was a boy broke through as a plover called overhead. Wyman and I had sat on an island point one September afternoon and whistled in plover. We shot some of them, dressed and cooked and ate them, because they had been legal birds in Wyman's youth, and he had wanted me to know his memories. Capt. Ted, Peter, young Harry Steele, the Lesters, Scotts and Helmuths... each of the human spirits who had sensitized me to the natural world, who had educated and trained and filled me with an understanding of the elemental, each was there breaking the waters of my mind as my boat hung in time's September vortex.

I fished as ritual. The bass have brought me joy since May, and I knew this was their final offering for the year. Massed as they were, the fish were vulnerable. On every cast into the schools that I could see, bass lunged for the lure, almost as soon as it touched the water. I kept six — enough to feed my household at that evening's dinner, with four fillets to save for Sunday breakfast.

As the sun went down, time returned. A breeze moved across the bay, shadowing the luminous waters, the gulls began wheeling away toward their outer island roosts. A nearly full moon glowed cold in the east, a flight of 11 black duck whistled overhead on another migratory beginning. The bass still broke the surged and swirled around me, but the temporal droplet had hit reality and the September suspension shattered. Like the wild ducks, the souls of my past who had shared this evening wavered away toward the horizons of my memory, flickering and diminishing in the gathering dark.

28

By the time I reached the dock, the moon was an important presence in the sky and on the water. Its refracted shimmerings gave light, allowed me to see the shape of the mooring buoy, and to row the pram easily ashore. As I pulled the pram up on the float, a bass broke just at my feet and the chased herring scattered from the moonwater in a tiny flight of bright arrows, arching up and then falling back.

I made one last cast, caught one last bass — the first I have caught from the very shore of our new home. I unhooked the fish gently, held it for a second and said to it: "I just wanted you to know who is living here." Then I dropped it into the night waters, to slip away and out to sea, along with each of my other friends that I had been with on that serene September evening.

There are, I'm certain, places where November sparkles, but I have never found them. In reviewing my Novembers, I find they have always found me well north of the 40th parallel where their seasonal somberness is consistent and unmistakeable. There must be, somewhere on the other side of the equator, a land where Novembers are bright blue instead of gray; where they mark the start of a beginning, not the beginning of the end. I will go there, some day, if I can find the place, because I would like November to somehow be redeemed; otherwise I shall put it down as the one month of the year that is more to be suffered than enjoyed.

The first day of this November in Maine was a classic sample of timeless November memories. It was especially so because it was so different from October's last day — a collection of sun, singing sky, bright leaves and laughter. Yet no sooner had November scrawled its name across the calendar and moved in as the season's new tenant, but the October colors were smeared and the bright mood covered over with gray.

At the house, the frost-browned marigolds slumped to their death in a brittle garden; the grass of the lawn, cut only a few days before, lay limp, drained of all enthusiasm. The wildly climbing vine that had softened the barn's hard edges had been stripped by kids and the wind; there was no disguise for the realities of the

29

place. The first edge of November's cutting cold had lacerated every autumnal illusion and left me standing outdoors totaling the discrepancies of the buildings, instead of marveling at the magnificence of the setting, as I did so often during the summer.

Perhaps it is the reality of November that makes it unredeemable. Shorn of the hope that spring brings, without the riches of summer or the curving cover of winter snows, November reveals too much. Like an acquaintance who tells nothing but the blunt truth, no matter how crass and how often, November allows for too little romance to ever be loved.

As I stood acknowledging the gray realities of November 1, I could see for the first time just how many panes were missing from the upper barn window. The blackness of the openings was jagged, crude and an insult to me as a caretaker. If I turned away from the barn, I faced the meadow. There the hay I had never gotten cut had become a browning mess of lumps and tangles that will reproach me until the snows. The pony wandered in a corral fast being scraped of any feed; soon it will have to come to the barn and be added to the list of daily chores. Under the shadowless gray sky, the house itself became an aging lady caught in an unflattering light. Every flaking scale of old paint was noted, every shoddy clapboard seemed to pop from its summer hiding place.

I stared out the window, not looking at anything except the marching of November's gray legions across my dreams. Beyond the meadow, the bay lay still, unrippled by any breeze — a banner of gray silk fallen from the low gray clouds. The sea will be flat, I thought, remembering my friends who are still fishing, and suddenly seeing them setting their nets in a gray, still Atlantic on this November day.

"Wait for 'Lection Day," the old ones used to say whenever the striped bass had not flashed past the beach in their final, surging migration; for Election Day was the traditional November time when most of the schools of fish that had been feeding in the tides of October gathered their millions and began the trip south. And it is true that November is the time when the striped bass makes his way along Long Island's surf, moving south toward the beaches of New Jersey and the eventual winter sanctuary of Chesapeake Bay. But it is also true that November brings the storms that kept us ashore as spectators while the striper schools flashed foamy white in the water. Waves too huge for boats to conquer rose between us and the fish, and we could only stand and watch the season's big haul go by.

Yet there was one Election Day dawn I can remember when the air was caught cold and motionless between gray clouds and a dark sea. There was no sun that early morning when I ran up over the dune to see if a prior storm had been gone long enough for us to fish. The swells were still tall, sharp and strong, but a good boat could crest them. They looked large from the dune, and as I measured their risk, I saw the fish that made every risk necessary.

It was the total bass migration. The countless fish were moving in a river of splashes and swirls along the surf's very edge. I ran back to the house to telephone the four other men of the sleeping crew, and none of us could move as fast as we wanted in that November dawn. We could not get boots on quickly enough, nor could we load the net, start the motors, pull all together. But when we did, the fish were still there, and in spite of the crashing seas, we filled the net with the biggest haul of the year.

Some of those men are still fishing this November 1 — a day of still waters — and I wish them well. They, and the fish they seek, are my only November redeemers.

In the last days of November, the ocean water temperature was warm enough to keep bluefish happy long after they normally decide to head south. I don't recall ever having heard of bluefish being off New England after Thanksgiving, but in this year of fine weather phenomena, I find the news entirely credible. After all, if the sun shines almost every summer day, the water it shines on has got to get warmer. (Which unscientific reasoning probably has absolutely nothing to do with offshore water temperature; but is strictly my own.)

In spite of gentle Novembers and their effect on chickadees and bluefish, by the time December rolls around Maine people had better begin to make ready for winter, or suffer some consequences. There is just no way to get out from under the reality of cold mornings yet to come, snow storms yet to howl, pipes yet to freeze, noses yet to run and cars yet to unstart just when you need them most. The cold is part of Maine. It is bracing, clarifying, beautifying and challenging, and it makes the change of the seasons ever so stimulating. It can also be as aggravating as the mosquitos of summer.

The way to avoid mosquitos is to wear lots of Woodsman's Friend; the way to avoid the aggravations of winter is to prepare for them. After twelve Maine winters, I consider myself almost ready. The chinks around the bottom of the house have been found and filled so various drainage pipes can not be frozen by the sly fingers of January nor'westers trying to see what mischief they can make once they break into the cellar. Missing window panes in the barn have been replaced so blowing snow won't drift around stored outboards and lawn mowers. Storm doors broken by kids and dogs have been repaired and put on and I even have snow tires already at work.

I don't yet know what to do, besides pray, that the car will start on those inevitable below-zero mornings. There was a time when I had all manner of machinery to help. I had electric gadgets plugged into long extension cords so I could insert heating elements into the engine block. I had huge plastic tents swaddled around the cars so I could put blower heaters underneath and pretend it was June in January. I sometimes tried running the engines most of the long night; and at one time I considered extending the living room so the car could be driven in. Finally, the insanity of my compulsion to leave home on a cold morning became clear. Now I do nothing special to the car; and if it won't start, I stay where I am, assured that the world's day has a fair chance of getting underway on schedule, even without me.

The common cold is winter's final reality that I have been unable to conquer, but I have been hard at work for the past several years and now consider myself near victory. People close to me, like my family and the office staffers who must endure me every day, know about my battle and have wearied of my endless propaganda on behalf of fresh oranges and Vitamin C. If it hadn't been for Dr. Linus Pauling and all the talk about his new book, I never would have had the courage to mention it publicly. But according to the *New York Times, Newsweek* and just about every other newspaper or magazine I picked up last week, Dr. Pauling says large doses of vitamin C will prevent and treat the common cold.

I've been saying that for years. The trouble is, I wasn't doing enough about it. At first, I took a vitamin pill or two on a casual and irregular basis. I still caught cold. Then I took the low-dose pills on a regular basis and started drinking orange juice almost every morning. I still caught cold. Then I discovered that fresh orange juice has infinitely more power than canned or frozen or processed, so I started buying oranges by the case, much to the delight of my peddler friend Harry Glovsky, who has never had such an orange customer. I even bought a super squeezer and consider my day ruined if I don't start with an eight-ounce glass of fresh juice.

I did that all last winter, and still caught cold — in fact, I had the worst case of the flu on record. It only made me more determined. This year, even Harry Glovsky can not believe the amount of orange crates carried through our door, and this year three vitamin C pills the size of a half-dollar go down with each morning goblet of juice. And if I see an odd vitamin pill lying around during the day, I pop that too. I gave up smoking three Novembers ago, so there is absolutely no reason why I shouldn't get through this winter without a cold — not unless Glovsky gives up his route.

Now that December is here, the Cole-Pauling theory of how to cure the common cold will be put to the chilly Maine test. If we succeed, I promise to let you know next May. If we fail, I'm certain someone on the staff will announce it. Meanwhile, in spite of the late-staying bluefish, you'd best get about your winter chores.

When we were striplings, my brother — who has been a painter ever since childhood — did a fine watercolor and titled it "Spring Light." I have never forgotten that painting, although I haven't seen it now for years. It was done during the first week in April on the far eastern end of Long Island (N.Y.). The scene was an open meadow, a white frame house and a towering bare elm tree which dominated the landscape. What makes the painting so memorable for me is the contrast of light and shadow created by the brilliance of the April sun shining with unblemished intensity through the clean spring air. Somehow, with untutored precision, my brother captured the essential quality of this seasonal purity and made it an unmistakable part of the painting.

Until I saw that landscape, I had never recognized the exceptional nature of the light we get in these latitudes in late March and early April. Since seeing it, I take note of the phenomenon every spring. As the years have gone by, I have gathered bits of information to enrich my comprehension of the event. Did you know, for example, that here in Maine we get more sun than most places in the northern hemisphere; and that it shines with the same intensity that it does in Florence, Italy. "Sunny Italy," as it has long been known, has produced some of the greatest artists of the ages, partly because of the light that enhances their work. Maine has the same sun.

You must have noticed it during the week just past. After four days of rain — which washed the air as well as soaking the ground — the northwest wind blew every cloud from the sky. The sun, now less than ten weeks away from reaching its annual zenith, rises before six and is already high in the sky by 10:30. Because there are no leaves on the trees, no foliage on the ground and no pollen particles or summer haze, the light is brighter than it ever will be again until the next April.

The light becomes the primary presence of the day. Seen in reflection and refraction on the surface of wind-shattered waters, the light leaps up in brilliant shimmers that blind every beholder. Pouring in through household windows in a spring flood that breaches every barricade, the light surges through rooms that become soaked in its revelations. Winter dark corners burst open; hallways where ghosts lurked on snowy dusks are sparkling avenues.

Outdoors, there are no shadows, only cool islands in a sea of diamond light. Branches without leaves do nothing to soften the sun; fields stripped of wildflowers by the glaciers of March can not diffuse the wash of light that plays over them as if the skies had opened. Every mote that can ever be seen by the eye of man is made visible; the light probes, presses and persists. It is hurled back into the eyes of every passerby from every puddle and swale; it illuminates, bounces, reflects and jumps from every bright surface as if it were chased by the forces of darkness.

Now, on these few days of spring light, less is hidden than ever before or after. Houses that take shelter behind a curtain of trees suddenly seem to jump out. "I never knew that place was there," says the traveler on a Maine road, newly transformed by the showers of light that fall in its rain-washed surface. Spaces that formerly seemed smaller and perhaps friendlier now appear vast and without dimensions. The patterns of the town streets that were so familiar are stretched by the strength of the light; they become other places with distant horizons, at once awesome and exciting. Elms and maples that soon will canopy and shelter are now mere shapes twisted in the light, and the reassuring perspectives of the softer seasons are moved back, like scenery moved offstage, leaving only the arc lights to shine.

In this undisciplined brilliance, man might find his own imperfections too harshly exposed. The light, after all, might seem so intense as to be without mercy. But this is not so. Something in nature's ways modifies the spring light's probings — not physically, but emotionally. I think it has something to do with the sun's function. It is being so lavish with its light because this superlative and unrestrained surge is needed to renew life in every bud, root and bulb.

Crushed by winter's weight, paralyzed by frost's harsh grip, the grass and trees and shrubs and plants might never stir from their deep sleep were it not for the bright shock of April's surging sun. So it is not to reveal our imperfections that the spring light flows, but to restore life to sun-starved plants. Somehow, we can sense this. We can feel the force under our feet. So rather than see our mistakes standing naked in the brilliance, we see the greening that will come so soon, shading us and our streets from ourselves, each other, and this spring light.

Last summer was so splendid that it carried me right through November. I kept close to the summer's warm memories the way a cat curls around a stove, finding contentment in residual warmth long after the embers have darkened and the fire has gone out. I knew I would have to move away from summer sometime, but I kept hoping the season's momentum might carry me through this winter, propelling me into spring and boat launching time before I even realized the bays had been frozen.

But now that winter is here, I have joyfully let go of summer and find new pleasures in the same places. It is the snow that made the transfer possible. If the dun ground were bare, the fields undrifted and the rooftops exposed...if all the trees were stripped and the barren land frozen but unblanketed, then I would try to pry my way back into summer to make winter bearable. But with the snow, winter becomes welcome.

Many of you will disagree. I know people who have a kind of snow phobia; they panic when they learn of approaching storms; they complain when the first flake falls; they sigh every time they must pick up a shovel to clear a path. For them, I feel real sorrow. They are missing the most of Maine's winters. If they are so preoccupied with snow's inconvenience, they never notice its beauty. Yet that beauty is incredible, more of a transformation than spring's first fragile green, more powerful than the lush crest of summer, more striking than autumn's frosty colors.

Traveling by car, on foot, snowshoes or cross country skis through any sparsely settled part of Maine almost always reveals scenic vistas unobtainable in most places of the world; but traveling just after a fat fallen snow like the one on Christmas Eve is another total experience far removed from lesser panoramic pleasures. As the light of the short days changes, as the sun makes its hasty trip across the southern edge of the winter sky, the quality of the snow itself takes on different character and color.

It is pale orange and pink in the reflected promise of the sunrise; it becomes blue snow instead of white in the sun's open rays when the sky is clear; and in the evening, the snow is violet as the sun sets. Only under cloudy skies, when more snow is about to fall, is the open snow white, the way it is thought to be always. Sometimes, if there is a snowfield between you and a cloudless sunset, you can watch the snowedge set afire as the red sun touches an icy torch to the rim of the frozen ridge and starts the crystals ablaze. If there is a moon to rise, the snowfires linger through the night.

Because it is so bright, the snow gives away the creatures who would otherwise be able to hide before your eyes. Without the cover of the underbrush, the partridge in our woods are suddenly and surprisingly visible. I have been passing their family gatherings all summer and fall, unaware of the splendor of their ways. But with the snow, I can see the birds from down the road. I can pull alongside them, slowly in the car because they are unafraid of the four-wheeled shape, and watch them move so close I could touch their feathers if I leaned from the window. They are such handsome birds, so at ease with their environment, like a lord in his castle. They are regal, proud, assured of their place in the winter as they step slowly along the roadside, unhurried and unharried. Their feathers are rich, their eyes bright, their feet sure as they draw them up quickly, and then extend them ever so slowly in that comic partridge step. I know that the birds will have to work harder to find food, but I could never guess it from watching them. They are too proud to seem put upon, too beautiful in their winter plumage to communicate alarm. I have seen them now three mornings since the Christmas Eve snow, at least three birds, once all together, and I had never seen them there before, even though I drive the road every day.

As the snow reveals the partridge, it also covers our mistakes, our chores and our confusion. I can no longer see the vegetable garden plot that was only half prepared for spring; the work that should have been done in the backyard is no longer a daily reprimand when I look from the kitchen window. Now, instead of raw earth that needs to be spread and seeded, I see only a tall and graceful drift, stretching away from the house like an alabaster canopy draped at the doorstep. Set in the hard whiteness of the drift's rim are the tender tracks of our kitten, a monument to his first exploration of the wilderness at the back of the house.

Other animals besides the kitten leave other marks in the snow, and even from a car speeding along the turnpike I can see the deep hoof cuts made by a deer as he lunged from the woods, stopped, sensed the dangers of the highway and leapt, in a great and still visible scattering of snow, back to the woods again. Or, in the loft of the barn, where the barest powdering of the coldest finest snow has sifted through the cracks in a closed window, I discover the minute embroidery left by a meadow mouse scampering on tiny, chilled feet across the splash of snow spilled in from the snowsea that surges outside.

Without that snowsea, my winter would be too barren to bear. With it, I can let go of last summer and cruise happily through this Maine winter, knowing I will reach safe harbor with the winds of spring.

It's been a bit chilly lately. Ever since the start of 1970, in fact, the temperature has hunched down below the thaw level and Maine has stayed frozen hard. We haven't had much snow yet in this part of the state (in spite of my maximum efforts) and I'm sure the frost line must be moving further and further down into the earth.

For the past week I've been starting the car before breakfast so it can warm while I'm eating, and that warm-up procedure is something I do only when the thermometer tells me the morning is in the minus degrees. We've had about four below-zero mornings in a row now, and I'm beginning to think it may yet become a cold winter.

So far, though, I haven't been really cold. I have felt the coldness, but it hasn't invaded me. It has been the kind of cold that I look for in a Maine winter: clean, sharp and charged with a presence electric enough to let a man know immediately that without proper protection, he could die of freezing. It is that sub-surface ripple of danger that makes a walk in the cold so extraordinary. And working outdoors for more than an hour becomes also a contest with the cold as well as exercise for flabby limbs.

I shoveled about a half-inch of snow off the skating pond one evening last week, doing most of my work in moonlight. The night was windless, but as I worked I knew the cold was there. I could tell by the way the inside of my nostrils frosted on a quick intake of the chill air. I could feel the tingle of numbness in the tips of my ears and the end of my nose; and if I stopped for too long in my work, the embrace of the cold slipped under my coat with sinuous and persistent fingers.

Because I stayed there in the sparkling dark until I got the pond clean, I felt the warmth of work and pride as I walked back along the hard, frosty road that led to the house with its lights and life inside. It was good to learn when I went in that the thermometer read 5° below. That's cold, especially when there is no sun; but, you see, I had not been cold. Instead, I was enlivened by the Maine night. My blood raced, the air was clean, rare and intoxicating; and I had stayed warm inside the cocoon of my coat and my activity.

That is not my idea of being cold, and I think too many people out of Maine have the wrong impression of what it is like here when they hear the TV weathermen read news of below zero readings in this state. If you are in New York City, where it may be a chilly 18°, you are likely to think that you're lucky when you learn it's eight below in Bangor. But the truth is that 18° in New York is wretched, while 8° below in Bangor can be a kind of delight.

No, my idea of being cold comes first with the northeast wind. Being cold is when you can not get warm, no matter where you go, or what you do, and that happens here on our coast and in our latitudes when the northeast wind blows its bitterness off the gray Atlantic. I heard a radio weatherman say the other day he didn't understand why the report always included wind direction. "Do people really care which way the wind is blowing?" the announcer asked, and it seemed obvious to me that he must have spent his life inside an air-conditioned, sound-proofed radio studio. For if he had been out in a northeast wind, he would have known what coldness is, and I don't think he would have forgotten it, or failed to recognize the meaning of wind direction.

A northeast wind is cold even in summer. Perhaps you can recall a day on the beach, or in a boat, when you quite suddenly became chilled to the bone by a silent change that caught you off guard and sent you scurrying for a sweater. If you had looked at a weather vane, you would have seen that it was a new northeast breeze that had brought you the cold.

Given the clouds that it usually brings, and the dampness that follows in its wake, the wind from the northeast makes warmth impossible. If you are unlucky enough to be aboard a boat when the wind change comes, then there is no escape from its misery. Those are my times of coldness — the ones I compare to when below zero talk makes everyone think it's cold. All I have to do is think back to the northeast days, and I know what base cold is — the cold from which all other chills must begin.

Because there is no comfort in the northeast wind. There are no clothes that can become a cocoon of warmth, no homes that can keep out the chill, no fires that can fight back the dampness, no corners where I can huddle to keep out of the wind. All that can be done is to muster enough stubborn bravery to be able to pretend that the northeast wind is not blowing. Some of my fishermen friends can do this. They can be on a boat, or a beach, or on the dunes mending nets, and they can stand there in the cold all day without giving in, without even an acknowledgment of its misery.

Their stoicism always showed me up. I could not pretend it, no matter how I tried. After working an hour or so in a nor'east chill, I would have to curse the weather, to shiver, sniffle and complain. In the end, I would become so enraged at the wind's relentless chill that I would leave, even though my fishermen stayed on. I would go inside and sit by the stove, trying for a warmth I could never find and had not earned.

That is what I call cold.

The snow that arrived Sunday was one of the season's finest gifts. There was more in it to be given than a base for a skier's enjoyment, although that is one of snow's more important blessings. No, the snow was of real importance because it made winter ring true as a season, and winter is a time Maine people can enjoy as few others can.

Who yearns for the sands of summer when the pond in the meadow is frozen crystal and a skater can glide across its transparency as he would step across the top of the world. And who longs for the sight of growing grass when gleaming fields roll quicksilver in the moonlight into a night so cold and pure the snowflakes shatter.

Let there be each season in its place, and let's have done with complaints about winter. It is the great challenge of the year, and we are all better for being tested by it. When else can a walk down a country road become a wrestling match with the elements, and when else does the icy air in the lungs speak so clearly of the delight of merely taking a breath.

There is such purity and simplicity to it all. The one crow in the white waste; the silent tides coursing under the bay ice; the sameness and symmetry of the leafless trees; all speak with the piercing silence of winter.

Try to find a place where winter comes as honestly as it does in Maine. It will do you no good to look in the cities or search the suburbs of the rest of the northeast; there they consider winter too elemental to be endured and so have shamed it with soot, slush and smog. In this part of the world, only Maine gives winter the welcome and the worship it should have. Because it requires liveliness, winter makes all of us feel most alive, and knowing the sense and wonder of being alive is a true and important wisdom. This winter gives us, and winter was here with the snow on Sunday.

By Monday, water had returned to the landscape.

It runs in the bright rivulets along the roadside, taking with each drop a part of its parent snowbank. Thin fingers of open water trace dark lines across the ice which covers the region's rivers, harbors, and bays. Where the tide runs swiftest, the jagged teeth of ice have lost their bite, their edges dulled by the surging of sub-surface water.

In gravel driveways and dirt roads, water turns the once frozen earth to mud; and far underground water flows high enough to be reached by the roots of winter-parched trees. Sweet water creeps under the maple's bark, and syrup takers hang their buckets to catch the sugary drops.

Bays and rivers are still white. Smelt shacks have yet some time to rest on their ice foundations. No boat owner, however eager, has his craft poised for launching. Ice fishermen still plan weekend trips. But long before spring arrives the return of water gives courage to all who must face the false springs of March and April.

During these months water will be at work. The millions of tons of ice which covers the Kennebec, the Androscoggin, the Abbacadasset, the Cathance, Muddy River, Maquoit Bay, Middle Bay, the New Meadows River and Hen Cove will be wiped away. Where, for so long there has been white, there will be blue. If you do not watch it carefully you will never see the change. You will only see suddenly that the bays and rivers are moving brightly instead of standing in white silence.

First, there must be at least three weeks of sub-freezing January weather; second, there must be little or no snow during that same time span. These conditions will produce a foot-thick stretch of bare, or nearly bare, ice on the bay that lies at the end of the road where I live. Then there must be one day of freakish January rain — the kind we had just last week. And immediately after the rain, the cold must come back for at least two days — long enough to freeze solid the layer of rainwater that lies like a sheet across the gray bed of bay ice. Finally, low tide must come in the middle of the day so the entire ice mass rests on the mud flats and I can skate its fantastic five-mile length without worrying about falling through an air pocket, or into a chasm forced by silent, sub-ice currents.

If each of these fairly incredible elemental events takes place in this even more incredible circumstantial sequence, and, in a final incredible fillip, the day on which it all culminates happens to be a day when the sun moves brightly through wild cloud patterns and a soft breeze hints at spring, then you have a day of bay skating that may occur once every century. Saturday was such a day and for myself, Sam and Tracy, two of the boys and a friend; it was marked in memory even as it was lived. Alone on that vast expanse of sheer ice that stretched to the horizon of the open ocean, we knew, even the youngest of us, that we were living a rare few hours; and we also knew that of all the millions upon millions of souls in the world, we were among less than a score blessed with the infinite natural treasure left at our doorstep.

The ice was so hard and smooth that when we looked at the bay from our windows across the meadow, it seemed as if we were seeing water. The sheerness of the chilled satin reflected every aspect of the sky above; and even the gull's flight was mirrored in the ice the way it would be on a still and bright summer day. But it was not still water that we saw — it was water frozen so quickly and silently that it retained all its unfrozen visual qualities. Skating over it was a breath-taking experience because the smoothness of the surface played optical tricks, making the skater's heart pound with fears that he was about to skate into open water — but always the illusory water became more of the incredibly smooth ice, and the skater glided further and further, sometimes on ice so perfect that not a sound came from the blades.

Our rink of perfection must have included at least thirty square miles. I made what I am certain is the longest hockey shot in history when I sent Sam a pass that traveled at least three-quarters of a mile. It could have been a mile, or more; I had only to skate further away before sending the puck skittering in endless motion across the glass beneath. But Sam looked so small, standing there waiting patiently in the center of the soaring expanse that I could not believe I could still send the puck to him across all the openness between us.

Skating alone, looking down at the ice, I was seeing the sky go by in reflected perfection. As the sun moved through the clouds, both sun and clouds moved under me, on the ice. Skating so smoothly, it was as if I were standing still, while the sky revolved above me and the earth turned beneath my feet. To add to the illusory enchantment were the colors of the late afternoon — the blues and the yellows and the oranges of the western sun; and along the shore the dark green pines bordering the aquamarine ice masses which had pushed from fissures in the rock cliffs that edge the bay.

And there we were in the middle of it all. A total experience of solitude in a world that could have been the same a hundred centuries ago, except for the planes that sometimes rumbled overhead, or the sounds of cars that came to us from time to time. But otherwise, in an earth full of people fighting for room to breathe and clean air to do it with, we were alone in time and space — little dots of souls moving across the ice desert the way small figures move in the perspectives of surrealist paintings. Our air was clean and sharp, our world so vast, so fresh, so wild, so open that we never strayed too far from each other, thinking perhaps that quite suddenly we had become the world's only souls. The afternoon was a totally exhilarating and religious experience. Sad, in a way, that no one else thought to enjoy it.

That night I expanded the bay's dimensions by designing the conversion of Bob's bobsled into a kind of ice boat, using the dory's sailing jib and making minor structural modifications — like the addition of a mast. Sunday morning Marsh and I got the job done with surprising success and pulled the strange rig down to the bay. The weather had warmed somewhat, and the ice was softer than the day before; but the place was still wonderful — except for one thing: there was not the slightest breath of wind to move our iceboat (?) to new adventures. We waited all afternoon, but the wind never came.

Now I wonder when, if ever, the same incredible set of elemental circumstances will occur again; for when it does, the iceboat will be ready. Meanwhile, we have the icy treasures of the skating days stored away for all of time future, and that is gift enough for a lifetime.

The ice went out of the bay last week; and I was there one afternoon to watch some of it leave with the falling tide. Afterwards I decided there can be few other natural events, if any, which are such dramatic witness to spring's arrival. Any Maine person who lives within sight of any water—stream, river, pond, bay or lake— has something of a seasonal edge on the land-bound; for without the ice-out to prove it, winter's end can too easily be prolonged.

I watched the ice move in last November. In the early mornings when I woke and looked out, I could see a slick on the still surface of the sheltered waters of the cove. I thought at first it was merely a place unruffled by the morning's light winds; then, as the sun warmed the night's frost, the slick patches would drift out into the bay like oil. I learned then that the rounded slicks were circles of early ice, too thin to survive the sun and the tides, but working each night for more of a hold.

One morning, the cove ice held fast against the tide and was still there in the late afternoon. By December, the cove was immobile, and the outer edges of the ice probed the open bay. Late in that short, dark month, the wind howled for two days and nights from the northwest, bringing with it an Arctic cold. When the wind let go and the night sky cleared, the ice leapt across the entire bay and locked in the surging waters. What had been wind-tossed blue water the day before was now lifeless, little more than a flat extension of the land, without trees.

Everywhere the eye could see, the bay was white. Even with binoculars, the far horizon of the open ocean was nothing more than a blue line between sky and ice. The gulls and sea birds that had defied winter with their life at our water's edge had gone, all of them, leaving the house with nothing but the chickadees and jays—land birds. The ice completed the silence of winter; it muffled every sea sound and subdued all movement.

As the snows gathered, the frozen bay became a white desert where the wind cut dunes from the drifts and blew the snow like sand across the hard dry ice. Then, in January, came a short thaw. The snow swept away and the ice surface was cleaned. It froze clear again, and we could skate for miles across the glistening skin. Still, skating is a winter sport; there was no sense out there that underneath the bay moved with the moon.

The ice stayed so long that we almost forgot the bay had been there. Winter had become too real. Putting on the big coat every morning became habit, and the acceptance of the cold beyond the door became routine. We began to think of life as always being congealed, indoors, snow dusted and sharp.

But in February's last days, all that changed. The thin blue line on the horizon grew wide. The circling gulls that watched over the ice edge could be seen without the glasses. And in the first week of March, overnight, a ribbon of water ran through the ice from our shore across the cove. At first it was more a string than a ribbon—a thin line of gray against the white ice. It widened to ribbon after one warm morning, became a sliver of open water just too wide to jump, although no one could tell how it had grown, so slowly did the widening take place.

That afternoon last week, as I was watching, the water ribbon became a breaking place. The acres of ice on the bay side of the gap began to move away, to slip down the bay with the first nudges of the falling tide. One field of ice—and it could have held a farmhouse, a barn and a potato lot—moved enough to be seen. I could line up an edge with a tree on the point and then watch that edge slip out of sight behind the trunk. The great gray ice mass moved quietly, and behind it was the sudden softness of open water, tickled by the wind, capped here and there with smaller floes and ice cakes, each one drifting away on a final solo voyage to the distant sea.

Even as the ice moved, the birds returned. When the ice-out tide had finished falling and the flats came out for their first day since November, the gulls and ducks swirled over them in a feathered rain. Their cries and callings broke the long winter's silence with a surge of sound that could be heard a mile away. It was as if spring had arrived in a few afternoon hours, and that sort of seasonal turning is not like Maine, who holds her winters tightly, letting go ever so slowly, from March to May.

At least that's what I had learned to live with until that afternoon last week. Now, after watching the ice leave the bay, and knowing that it is gone for good, I can take whatever March has left to give. That's what I mean when I say that Maine people who live by water have an edge.

Maine makes us wait so long. Each year I tell myself not to think about it, but to move through April on determined tracks that allow no longing. Yet, after more than a decade of these waits, after more than ten Aprils of honing my determination, I find this spring more excruciating than ever.

This April is more painful, I tell myself, because there has been no snow. In most of my other Maine springs, the compress of the winter snow has shielded the land from the wrenching freezes and thaws that so mark this spring. Never once sheltered by the protective embrace of deep snow, the lawns and fields have gone naked through this winter, and it has ravaged them. The total lifelessness of their March is still with us, for without snow the fields are dun dead seas, lying becalmed, colorless and defeated. Try as I might, I can find no single sliver of green in all the acres of meadow that can be seen from the roads to and from my house. Nor can the ponies snuffle up one spring mouthful, even though the spring sun shines when they wander across the dun seas in search of just one green island.

Waiting for the green through March was bad enough, but waiting through April is hell. It is, perhaps, the mud that insures the hellishness. Merely sere fields might bring a kind of pathos; it is the mud that brings the pain. Bereft of snow, the fields can not be run in or walked on; the lawn can not be worked, cleaned or played on — unless the man who sets foot on field or lawn wants to feel the earth's skin slide away with each step. Still frozen in its deep body, the earth's snowless skin has been warmed just to thawing. It is a cruel warmth — like that of Florida sun burning an old man who is dead and cold inside.

Every shoe or boot that touches the meadow feels the turf slide away. Every child's step on the lawn where they played last summer and want to begin again is a small knife slicing through the brown grass mat. Every one of man's movements across the unpaved outdoors is the opening of an earth wound that bleeds brown mud. It blots the children's knees and elbows, it soaks shoes and boots, clings to dog haunches, splatters car fenders, and is cast off in gritty chunks throughout the entire house. First wet and chill, then abrasive and ugly, the mud of this spring has made me lose patience with Maine waiting and cry for the warmth which can heal the earth and close the mud wounds.

The Maine waiting. Is there any other place where it lasts as long? I don't think so; for if it lasted longer, spring would never come, and there would be no expectations. It is hope that keeps us waiting — a hope built on the bittersweetness of the first flight of wild geese on the winds of March, the first call of the redwing, the running of the sap, the breaking of the bay ice, the longer days, the softer storms and the first wasp, clinging desperately to a false start in the inside sunlight of the kitchen windowsill.

We are all there, clinging and waiting. We are stiff with winter. We are cold and coldy, sniffling, coughing, hoping and waiting. We want those open, dry, warm days when the earth crumbles dark in our working hands instead of running wet in bleeding rivers of mud. We yearn so. We search so for any sign that the waiting will end. We cannot live in the cruel present; we live in dreams of the future and push those dreams until they are broken by brutal reality.

Marshall tries to work in the barn, but winter won't let his hands uncurl. The snow is gone, but the boats can't be painted because the March damp is too deep in their sodden wooden ribs. The lawn should be raked clean of its storm rubble, but even the flimsy fingers of the rake scratch like cat's claws. The old stone step we want to move to the front door can't be pushed into its final place because still more frost has yet to be unlocked.

And so we wait. And we step outside on this sunny muddy morning and there is the crocus, a small bright signal in the sun-warmed soil saying that if we can just wait somewhat longer, we will once again pass Maine's toughest test and know the joy of rolling on warm wet grass and living in a green world where every moment is revered because we had to wait so long for its coming.

The winter of '72 was noted for its false alarms, and its definite end came with the same sort of happy mis-direction which so characterized the entire over-advertised season. Every weatherman on the radio dial or television channel was warning the people of Maine on Friday, March 31 that a foot of wet snow was on the way to shock the Easter weekend. But instead of snow, Saturday washed us in bright warmth, covered us in drifts of spring's fragrant breezes. Instead of a late-season storm to greet me on the first

April morning, I awoke to the call of an early redwing.

It was an all-out day that held nothing in reserve. The kind of a day that tells every person, no matter how wary, that spring has not only arrived, but has conquered. It was the kind of day that allows no soul to live through it without making public testimony to its brilliance. Everywhere the thawing soil was soft, everywhere the melting snow made rivulets across the roads and everywhere men and women came out from under their eaves to look toward the sun, pick up a winter-broken branch from the yard, or walk coatless along the singing paths. Children fluttered free like kites in the wind and their chirpings drowned out the birds.

I had an errand which took me far from home, and under the influence of spring's whimsical ways, I traveled the very longest, most remote and rural roads to get where I was going. Slowed by the contorted roads of spring, which bucked, heaved and pot-holed themselves in their effort to wriggle free of winter's frozen clasp, I had much time for looking as I drove. With the snow about gone, no leaves on the trees, no bud yet burst to bloom, no green showing in any lawn or field, and with the new April sun undimmed by even the slightest cloud, all of the countryside was open to scrutiny, revealed in as much merciless detail as a surgeon's anatomical model under a floodlight.

The roads I chose were those I had never before traveled, and perhaps for that reason I was more aware of what I saw. But I think even the novelty of first sight was not the reason my trip is still so well remembered. I know I won't soon forget the journey because it took me too far into Maine's past, and left me too deeply shaken by how far from the dignity of that past so much of Maine has come.

Scattered along every one of the rural roads I drove, like grave-stones along a winding river bank, were the skeletons of aban-doned farms, stirred in the first spring sun by some ghost of a for-gotten farming time. I could hear the whinny of horses from under the tumbled beams of a falling barn; I could see the plow being drawn from the blackness of a gaping cellar hole; and on the buckled porches of the windowless gray buildings, I could watch the ghostly farm women walking with their day's wash on their arm, happy to have the warm sun to hang it in.

If ever there was a fine season for a farmer, spring it would have to be, especially in Maine. With the long winter gone, the cows coming to calf, and the fields soon ready to turn and sow, past springs must have come as a blessing to every empty place I passed. This day it came as a medium, calling for a visit from the souls of the departed farmers, begging for their return to shore up the sagging buildings, to fix the torn and leaking roofs, to build a fire in the cold and rusted stoves, to clear the bull briars from the barnyard, to move the ancient farm machines.... to restore a life and purpose to the once lovely, carefully crafted places that now stand alone, decaying in the solitary wind like some untouchable marooned on a deserted island.

These gray and lonely farms were once the strength of Maine; now they are nothing but so much rotting wood, land gone fallow, homes without inhabitants. The fields once cleared with a blister for every fencepost and a year for every five acres are still cleared, but the pines are taking hold, slowly, the way people fill a church for the earliest service. Soon the trees will take it all, and Maine will have forgotten the lives of dignity, independence and grace once lived on these fine farms.

But they cannot be forgotten yet; not when they scream so in the bright spring light. They shout that lives were once fulfilled on these farms, and never more fulfilled than in the spring. Further down the road, a man rakes the yard of his mobile home, or trims the fence in front of his one-story ranch-style. He is happy for the end of winter, but if he looks up and sees the derelict places, he must also weep for Maine's loss of its farmers' spring.

THE HOME FRONT

This began in my mind as a rhapsody to the first snowfall. That was last evening, driving home, when the snowflakes swirled in my headlight beams like cold sparks from a bonfire. The wind blew so hard across the open fields near the house that the road was black and bare. Then, in the woods where the high pines crowded both roadsides, the snow stayed where it fell and everything was white.

I loved it, and I was as excited as the children who had wrapped the ponies in blankets of burlap, as if the early December snow were a blizzard that threatened their pampered livestock. Sam threw the season's first snowball as I opened the door. I turned around, feigning revenge, and saw how fine the drab lawn looked covered by snow. It really belongs, I said to myself, and I'm glad to see it.

So when I awoke early this morning and watched how the rising sun hung its lights on every icy branch, I definitely decided the first snow should be noted here. I could do it properly too, because Sam's new schedule required his appearance for hockey practice at eight. That would leave me plenty of time to get the writing done before the day got busy.

I got Sam and his skates and sticks into my car, and the disintegration of my day began. The car would not start. The evening's snowy ride had slopped slush onto the manual choke (yes, it has a manual choke) cable, the slush had frozen, the choke was immobile, and without the choke on such a cold morning, starting was impossible. I upped the hood, fiddled with the carbuerator, looking for ways to free the choke. I failed, I felt my temper going. It went. I roared with rage at the futility of dealing with inanimate, frozen cold machines.

Sam was now late, and after we had gotten such an on-time breakfast, I could not stay stubbornly—as I wished—and make my car go. I had to give up and take to the big car, the family car, the number one clumsy that I don't often drive. It started, Sam and I went down the bejeweled road; the sun was brighter, and I felt my temper sliding away and my joy restored by the incredible fragility of the morning. Yes, I thought, I can still write the rhapsody.

We had gone about two miles when the car ran out of gas. One of the boys had borrowed it the night before to drive home a young lady. And, as the boys seem able to do almost every time, this one had returned the number one vehicle with a pint of gas in the hollow tank.

Again I roared. This time with more reason. I had run out of gas precisely one week before in the very same spot on the very same errand. That time, I was in my little car, and it ran dry because it had been drained the previous evening by one of the boys who felt it was permissible to siphon all the gas from the old man's car. I had explained rather forcefully that the boy had made a fundamental error of judgement; and now, one week later, I was out of gas again because of the same boy.

I found it easy to start walking to the nearest gas station; difficult to be civil to the kind person who gave me a ride. At the gas station-general store there were no extra cans for me to take fuel back to the car. I telephoned home and roared into the phone that one of the boys had better come to my rescue or face the prospect of Christmas in a wheelchair.

Then I walked back to the gasless car where Sam waited, wondering if his hockey team would play all morning without him.

After a fifteen-minute wait for one of the boys to make a two-mile trip, Sam and I were still unaided. Officer Murdock of the local constabulary solved the most pressing problem when he saw us, kindly offered his assistance and gave Sam and me a ride to the hockey rink, thus saving what was left of Sam's game. As I left the rink I was met by one of the boys driving my car, the one I had left at home with a frozen choke. The boy was grinning, shifting through the gears and generally enjoying himself. If it hadn't been for Officer Murdock, bones might have been broken.

As it was, I thanked the policeman, got in my car with Chris and had him drive me back to the gasless and abandoned vehicle. "How did you get this started?" I inquired, knowing in advance the answer would reduce me to the rank of harmless cretin. "Oh, nothing to it," came the jaunty reply, "Marsh looked under the hood, saw the choke was frozen, did something with his fingers, put the hood down and started it right off.....Say, you know this little thing really does well on these icy roads." Whereupon, he down-shifted, threw the car into a controlled skid around a downtown corner.

I could muster no more rage. An hour had gone. The snow on the roads was turning to slush that splashed me as cars whipped by where I stood filling the gasless car from a five-gallon can Chris had brought. It took another 20 minutes to start it. I drove it to the gas station, filled the tank and the five-gallon can brimful, turned the car over to Chris, retrieved mine, and headed for the sanctuary of my office where I sat alone, whimpering.

This could have been a rhapsody. It was meant to be; it was planned. The first snow was perfect, right on time, right on target. It needed honoring, but not by a beaten man.

Considering the mental anguish it has caused, I am totally confused as to why we have planted grass seed on some part of our lawn for the past five springs. Oh, the mechanical reasons have been obvious. One year we had to repair the havoc created by the bulldozers, etc., when they made us a new drainage field, septic tank, etc. Another time we decided we had to have a door built where the dining room window had been. We needed it to help handle the traffic crisis created by a mob of teen-age giants; once the new exit was installed, the forsythia just outside it had to be moved and new grass sown. The most horrendous spring was the one when the entire small field of goldenrod, weeds and other wildflower delights was converted to a lawn because "someone" decided the children needed more space to play. It pains me to recall even the most fragmentary memory of that catastrophe.

There have been others almost as distressing, but somehow I thought I had seen the end of the miseries. No matter how hard I tried last autumn, I could find no patch of ground that needed further landscaping, and so I soared through the winter on dreams of a contented spring. I reveled in the anticipation of no more truckloads of topsoil (looom, as Mr. Larrabee calls it) avalanching onto the homestead, and I realized that in spite of the mechanical reasons we had found for our previous battles with grass seed, the psychological reasons must have been dark indeed—the mental suffering had been too intense for any reward but the rewards of pain (masochism, I believe it's called).

Now, I am convinced we seek out this pain because no sooner had the first 1970 peeper sounded his trembling, thin, wintery note, but I found myself blocked from my own driveway by a stampeding herd of Larrabee trucks, snorting, lurching and dumping more mountains of sand and soil at the very front door of the home I had considered so safe from invasion. I recalled having muttered something about more gravel for the driveway. Too many winters of snowplows had scraped at the strip, and most of its outer shell of larger gravel had been shoved onto the lawn.

I should have realized, of course, that my apparent wish to save the driveway from complete destruction was nothing more than a subconscious desire to once again impale myself on the delicious anxieties of grass growing. Of course! I should have known. Once Mr. Larrabee had given the driveway back its shell, he immediately realized he had also raised its level and would have to grade up the lawn along its edge so the drive would drain properly. And while he was at it "someone" said, why not fill in that low spot (about a quarter of an acre) in the front lawn that had been so bothersome. And, oh yes, we could also use some new soil and seed around the front door, and as long as you're here, I'll relocate the flower beds.

So now I enjoy 100 percent agony. There is a sea of mud stretching from my doorstep, flooding ground that I had always considered inviolate, shattering the once welcome feeling of security I used to get as I looked over the homestead from the front stoop each new morning. I have, as Zorba said, the full catastrophe.

And the elements have done their best to help it along. Last week's downpours really did a job. Whatever grass seed had been left by the screaming bird flocks (they follow the Larrabee trucks) was cascaded into tiny mountains by the freshets and floodlets that cut gullies and mini-canyons across the entire squishy stretch. For some reason, the dogs seemed to find the mud much more appealing as it gained in fluidity. Like actors and actresses leaving their mark in Grauman's cement, Tina, Heidi, Fanny, Hans, Rhody, Sport and a host of other famous neighborhood canine stars presented me with their footprints, not just once, but a hundred times. And the remnants of my old fish net (saved for sentimental reasons) that were used by "someone" to protect the front door landscaping only served as great stuff for the dogs to chase the cats through. The incredible succession of disasters was so defeating that I scarcely twitched as one of the boys was driven home by an engaging friend who laughed and waved as he backed out a good forty feet into the seeded mud sea before he realized his hub caps were no longer visible.

The problem is, you see, that I am now trying to get the grass to grow through the sheer force of my transferred kinetic energy. I can exhaust myself in five minutes just standing on the front porch, pouring out my concentrated "growth" thoughts at those microcosms of brown seeds lying so lifeless in the mud. None of you has any idea how much I want those seeds to sprout, nor how hard I try to get them to sprout by wishing it and willing it to happen. I may look as if I'm working, but I'm really thinking "GROW"; and I may appear to be writing for *Maine Times*; but, as you must have figured out, it's that damn grass seed that's on my mind.

When I came to Maine and first began country living, I never really planned to have anything but a most casual relationship with horses. My feelings toward equine society were not so negative that I would cross the street to punch any Dobbin in the nose; but my childhood had been so decidedly traumatized by the antics of several huge horses that I was definitely opposed to any action that would put me within smelling distance of the animals. (See an early *Maine Times*, this column, for the story of the horse that ate the buttons from my new overcoat.)

I hadn't counted on the opposing reactions of my daughters, and the daughters of others whom my sons admired. If my own female offspring were not forcing my attentions on horses, my male offspring were bringing home young ladies who never went anywhere, including our house, unless on horseback. Each time I heard that thundering "clop-clop" in the driveway I knew I would have to leave the safety of the house and go outdoors and be nice to some hulking grass-eater pulling up chunks of my new lawn.

But those horses never stayed overnight. Not until I was horse-traded out of my barn and into harboring two horses of dubious background for an entire year was I to learn the full extent of the suffering caused by dumb animals; and boy, these horses were dumb. I was jostled into the agreement by the slickest of grand-fathers, whose neighbors had begun to complain (although he never told me that) about the havoc being raised by the two horses he kept for his grand-daughter. Why didn't I take them, he said, and save the girl from tears, and also put my fine barn to some productive use. What can a parent say, especially when the girl in question also happens to be a good friend of a son.

No sooner had I said yes, but the horses arrived. Not only the horses, but truckloads of hay bales which were stuffed to the very rooftop of the barn, their bulk causing the old building to sag depressingly and tilt alarmingly toward the back pasture. It was still late summer, however, and the horses were able to spend most of their time staked in the meadow. Not until winter arrived did I realize the full enormity of my commitment.

For when the snow covered the pasture, the horses were confin-ed to their stalls. Down came the bales of hay, and out came the horse manure—the process of its manufacture seemed almost instantaneous and endless. By that time the son's ardor (toward both girl and horses) had begun to cool almost as fast as the thermometer dropped, and it took at least five minutes of full volume shouting to get him to take shovel in hand and head for the stalls. After he got there, he just skimmed the surface of the problem.

But just the surface stuff was enough to fill a roomsize bin I had built outside the barn just under the two holes in the building that opened on the horse stalls. The manure chute—as my struc-ture was politely called—was supposed to catch the results of Bob's inside cleaning. Instead, he hurled the horse apples with such anger that they often zoomed right over the chute and out into the garden, lawn, and every now and then, the driveway.

Enough, however, landed in the chute to collapse it quite totally shortly before mid-winter. For the rest of the winter, my sense of order was trampled daily by the sight of torn lumber, splintered posts, chaotic angles and a huge mountain of frozen-in horse manure steaming in the snow. I have often thought that if the horses had belonged to me, I might have shot them. (Except there's that story of the horse that died in a Harpswell barn and for too many days no one could be found to remove the body. Come to think of it, what does a civilian type do with a dead horse?)

I did not harm them in any way, but when spring came I paid a high ransom to have the manure hauled away, the lawn resodded and seeded, the garden unsoured, and the manure chute rebuilt by someone who knew what he was doing. I also got rid of the horses.

Ah, but my relief was short indeed.

No sooner had those horses gone but my youngest daughter decided she was old enough to have a horse of her own. Not only that, but her mother agreed with her. And not only that, but having just seen a re-run of "National Velvet" she built a Kentucky fenced corral in the meadow huge enough to hold all the entries in the Kentucky Derby. (It's so big, we later discovered, one fence line is on a neighbor's land, but that's another story too.)

Of course, the manure chute went back to work, but I could not stand the thought of another winter's strain, so we have been boarding the horse at a friend's real farm — as opposed to our pseudo one. But just the other day Tracy looked out the window at the green grass and said, "Hey, look at that. It's time for Brandy to come back." The thought ruined my breakfast; and one more summer may ruin my second manure chute.

When I came to Maine, I did not own a boat. Now I have four, and I wonder how I got into this alarming situation. It happened gradually, over a period of years—a kind of creeping marine growth, like the sea grass that sprouts on hull bottoms, silently and unnoticed until it slows the boat almost to a halt with its unwanted weight.

The first boat is not really mine; it is my responsibility and I get the pleasure from it, which, in a sense makes it mine. But, in actual point of fact, it is being held in trust for its rightful owner—a professor of comparative literature at Rutgers who also fights bulls and writes books. Perhaps some of you in Freeport remember John McCormick. He held the record for Maine commuters for a number of years with his weekly trips to Freeport from somewhere in the wilds of New Jersey.

He finally gave it up, or his wife and family persuaded him that it would be a better world if he kept the household in one piece. So he moved back to New Jersey, and before he left he entrusted unto me the lovely Swampscott dory that had rested bottom up on the McCormick front lawn for at least one summer. It was in excellent condition, needed only minor restoration, and has served me as a loving and beloved friend for five years now. From it have been cast the lines that caught the most exciting striped bass and the bravest mackerel; and from it has come the laughter of scores of different children who have found their summer's delight in a dory.

On top of all this, it can, and has, been sailed. One should think, I would imagine, that a fellow with such a craft would have no call to even look at another; and normally one would be correct. But about three years ago a little pram came my way that I just could not resist. Prams are those tiny, square-ended craft that sailing yachts keep perched on their stern so the captain can row himself to and from his mooring to the dock. This one had been on someone's rather splendid yacht, for it was trimmed with mahogany, built with the finest timber and fashioned with brass fastenings throughout. For $10, delivered, I could not resist.

Since then, the pram has been used rather brutally for such a dainty shiplet. The boys have caroomed around the bay in it, testing its ultimate limits by strapping a 3-horsepower outboard to the frail stern, and winding up the motor to top speed. On a six-foot pram, that is top enough. The smaller children have learned to row in it, and I use it in the fall to row out to the little island where I escape to in October to watch the ducks fly. The pram is the only boat light enough to be pulled across the flats when the low tide leaves me high and dry.

For awhile the pram and the dory made a lovely couple, and they slept arm in arm through the winter under the apple trees. When the snow melted and the apple blossoms burst, it took only a week or so to get the contented pair outfitted for the new summer season.

But now all that has changed. It began with last June's commotion about making a mint trapping eels. Between myself and the boys, we had a financial success story already written; but, among other things, we needed a boat for tending our traps. For several days, I pondered on using the dory, but I couldn't bring myself to turn such grace to the graceless task of hauling eel pots (or carrying the bait they needed). To spare the dory, my conscience and the memory of John McCormick, I began a search for an eeling boat. The hunt ended in a Bath boatyard where I resurrected—for about what the pram cost—an old working lady of such rugged years that she had a bruise on every rib and plank. I don't know why I brought the old wreck home, except that she reminded me of my old Emma, the original, flat-bottomed, 16-foot seafaring mistake which my grandmother bought at a Macy's sale and in which I spent my roughest days clamming and learning about the winter sea.

The old crone from Bath had the same lines, saved from the Emma's total ugliness by a hint of sheer in the bow which lifted my heart as it lifted the boat's character. It took some weeks of work to get the antique restored enough to launch. Every seam was open, almost every plank was sprung. But Bob socked several pounds of caulking to her, and she recovered enough of her battered aplomb to stay afloat in sheltered waters, even though she never quite gave up the leaking habit, and without a bailer would have swamped at some point in the day. As if to make up for her deficiencies, she turned out to be an easy rower, with hints of former nimbleness, even grace.

The fourth boat is not wooden; it's a small Boston Whaler, the first plastic craft I've ever owned, and, in this sense, a broken promise to myself. I have no excuse for buying it, except that it came to me second-hand in mid-winter as a bargain and I had been out in Whalers before and like the way they go and their safety and stability features. It's a fine boat; but I don't think I shall ever love it. That emotion seems to belong to the aging wooden ladies of the waterways who find their way to my landing whether or not I invite them.

For the past weeks, the two oldest boys have been thrashing around looking for a job. Their aimless journey through the limbo of unemployment at this late seasonal date began when Anguilla Corp. suffered a monumental setback. For that, I feel responsible; and also feel responsible for the two frustrated wage earners now darting here and there trying to find some way to make a buck.

Anguilla Corp. was the eel trapping and marketing scheme which I put together at great cost and which was supposed to earn the boys about $30 or $40 a week apiece. It didn't. We spent a month making eel traps, hanging a minnow seine to catch bait, and the rest of those long days being defeated by various elemental catastrophes which, in a final catastrophic cascade, led us to the acknowledgement of our defeat by the eels. Casualties were high on both sides.

Amont the wounds I suffered was a loss of my status as the "big fisherman". After watching me stagger through the mud trying to save a half-bushel of minnows that were escaping from our net, and then failing, the boys have become exceedingly sceptical about any further claims from me. They are gentle in their doubts. They don't just stand there and tell me they don't believe me. They listen quietly, and then walk away without response. It's their way of saying they think I exaggerate my prowess, and have done most of my successful fishing in my imagination; or in a youth so distant that its realities have been washed away by rivers of time.

So I never did try to persuade Marsh that he should try clam digging as a profit making occupation, or at least a temporary fill-in while he looked for more comfortable work. I thought it would be too much of an emotional burden for him to be asked once again to follow his father's advice to further commercial fishing frontiers. But he overheard me mention the idea, said he wanted to try, got together boots, clam rake, baskets, license and high hopes; and we headed for the clam flats early Saturday morning.

I had my old rake, and I was going to show Marsh how clamming is done, then leave him on his own to make enough money to buy a motorcycle. (Not on just one tide, you understand.)

I'm sure my exhilaration about clam flats reaches no soul but my own; yet I'm also sure even the most callous realist would have been stirred by the morning we found waiting for us. Fog wound around us, keeping us alone on the vast expanse of a drained bay, and we worked in a wet world of salt mud, warm wind and sea forms of overhwelming abundance. Herons stood at the edge of our fog-bound horizons like birds in a Japanese print, and terns cried invisibly beyond the mist where they chased silver fish in a pool the low tide had not emptied.

Against such a back drop, I was able to accept the grub work of taking a clam from his nest of rocks, mud and old shells. At the beginning I could live with the ache in my constantly bent back, the wrench of tendons as booted feet sank deeper into the black, sucking mud, and the discomfort of bitter sweat dripping into my eyes.

There was a challenge set up for me. I could not fail twice. And besides, the eeling had been experimental; clamming is one of Maine's venerable professions, and a score of men—young and old —make a living on the same flats Marsh and I were probing. So I was determined not to be defeated; although I did allow a possible honorable retreat by saying in advance that our goals should not be too high for the first day—after all, we had no idea where the best clamming spots would be.

The fog left us, the sun took its place, and how plaintively I wished for the fog to return. The sun was heavy and hot; it killed the life in the breeze, and, worse than that, it awakened the greenhead flies. Even the challenge of proving myself to my son could not keep me there at the mercy of the green-heads. With both my hands working the clam rake, my back bent and my shirt too thin to stop the flies, I was forced to shake and shout and curse as I felt the damned insects sink their biters into their favorite biting grounds just under my shoulder blades.

It was too much. Another ten minutes and I would have thrown myself down and rolled in the black mud. I quit; besides, the tide was on its way in and Marsh and I had a good half-bushel, enough for the first day. We walked back along the shore carrying the basket together, and I wondered if I should ever mention fishing or clamming again to anyone. Quite obviously, I said to myself, I am unbalanced about the topic. Besides, at that point you couldn't have gotten me back out on those flats for any amount of money.

But later in the day, after a rest and a shower, I was on the bay again, this time in a boat at high tide chasing mackerel. And this morning, I took Marsh back to the clam flats, to work alone because I had *Maine Times* chores to do. I looked at him walking into the fog, listened to the terns cry, and wished I could be with him, digging in the stinking mud, even though my back throbbed and my legs were still cramped from the day before.

On the first school morning, just after Sam and Tracy had run to catch the bus as I watched from the window, two chickadees popped down for a momentary tail twitch on the porch railing. I hadn't noticed any chickadees around the place during the summer and I thought their appearance on the first school day was more of a seasonal indicator than the bright yellow bus or the September dew on the children's new shoes. Chickadees are winter birds. They hang around the bird feeder during the most frozen moments of the snow, and they reach their peak of popularity when they become the only winged creatures of the winter—all others having flown south, leaving the chickadees alone to remind man that winter is not endless and spring will bring more song.

Seeing the pair on the porch reminded me that it was time to think about the bird feeder for this year, and the thought was not without its tendrils of dread. Ever since I left the parental roof, I have had a bird feeder of some sort outside of some kind of window of the place where I have lived. Most of the feeders have, however, brought me some form of misery: several have been the focus of real trouble. As I review the sorry history, I wonder if I shall try again this year.

One of the times I came close to getting shot, the threatener was upset about bird feeders, namely hers and mine. She was a nice neighbor lady type whom I never really met, but who could have won any town trophy as a typical NOL (nice old lady). She had a lovely home, tidy, well restored and charming. She and her NOL companion lived in quiet tolerance of a rather young and noisy neighborhood and gave homemade cookies to the kids every Halloween. She did not project the slightest hint of violence until my dog began eating her peanut butter and suet.

It was the peanut butter and suet, of course, with which the NOL larded her bird feeder. The dog, a big, bumbling combination collie-labrador, would amble over to the feeder in the early morning and stretch her big face up to the windowsill bird feeder and gobble the goodies before the NOL had a chance to scream. That was a big winter for grosbeaks, and what really converted the NOL to violence was the abandonment of her feeder by the town's grandest grosbeak flock.

A series of bitter phone calls began. In a short while I trembled at every ding-a-ling, so spiteful was the speech from the other end. The trauma worsened as I became forced to publicly punish my dog, under the NOL's scrutiny so she could be convinced that I did not take the matter lightly.

It was to no avail. Nothing I could do—including catching my dog in the act of suet nabbing—could stop the deprivation. The NOL called in the police, she threatened to shoot the dog, then me. I am certain the point of violence would have been reached if I had not abandoned the community altogether and moved far away.

Not too much later I reached a house blessed with the feeder of my dreams. The previous owners had been bird watchers and lovers and had conducted the kind of high volume, mass feeding operation only a government agency might consider. As a result, the feeder tree just outside the kitchen window looked like a series of Audubon illustrations. Even on bad days anyone could count at least six different species hopping just inches from the window pane. And on good days we got visits from such spectaculars as orioles, cardinals, fox sparrows and oven birds. I was entranced and delighted at the unexpected bonus, and quickly set out to eliminate the only problem—the feeder's location. Not hankering to be found too often in the kitchen, especially near the dish-filled sink where the window was, I moved the massive feeding assembly just a few feet to the west so I could watch it in quiet safety from the living room.

If I had only known. The living room window in the old farm-house was full size; it reached almost to the floor. In addition to the bird army, a red squirrel also dropped by daily for a go at the sunflower seeds. It was too much for the dog (yes, the same one) to see the squirrel chattering in all its impudence just beyond a pane of glass. Three days after I had moved the feeder, the dog charged across the living room and hurtled through the closed window, taking glass, frame, sash and all.

It was late October, and cold. It cost dollars that were sorely needed in those days to get the window rebuilt. Four days after the work was finished, the dumb dog pulled the same trick. I mov-ed the feeder back to the kitchen and inquired about insurance.

I have since left the site of that super-feeder, and the dumb, wonderful dog has left this world. Now i restrict myself to rather chintzy little feeders that hold a mere potful of sunflower seeds or a dollop of suet. It's not a big operation anymore, but it brings a few tough chickadees to the playroom window. They stay, chica-dee-dee-dee-ing in the snow, even though the cat murders one or two a month. The little birds are so spunky that I love them; enough so that after seeing the pair on the porch I'll go out and resurrect last winter's feeder and buy a bag of sunflower seeds — in spite of all previous disasters.

How long would a winter be without a chickadee?

A bit of water adds an immeasurable extra dimension to the life of a country dweller. A tiny pond, a thin stream, even a roadside ditch that fills during spring and autumn can be as big as an entire new world to the eyes of a country child; and adults who are denied access to water never quite escape the knowledge of their limitation. As for how some city people get through a lifetime without the blessings of water, I'll never know.

I am rich with water. There are two ponds by the house, and at the end of the meadow there is the bay that opens to the far ocean. Neither one of the ponds "belongs" to us, in the sense that we own the land around them, that belongs to our neighbors, one of whom lives in some distant city and seldom visits his Maine land; the others — a couple — do have a handsome house, but are in Maine for just a few weeks of the summer. Then they put up a miniature lighthouse at one end of the pond in the meadow, and a red light flashes in the tower to warn the peepers, the moose and the nesting ducks that the house is occupied by man.

That pond is the largest of the two, and deep enough and well fed enough to stay a pond even in summer droughts. The small pond to the west of our house dries up in dry seasons; and even when it's full it's not quite deep enough to prevent bullrushes from taking over its entire span. But the bullrushes provide a home for all kinds of lively and noisy creatures, and the Frog Pond (as we call it) is actually the most productive of the two. Teal have nested there each spring. Frogs and peepers of all kinds raise so much cain over there in the warm months that they actually frightened a fine lady from the city who came to visit us for awhile.

In May, frog and salamander eggs clutter the surface like gelatinous algae; and each spring for as long as we have lived here at least one of the children has gotten soaked in the Frog Pond in the process of trying to catch tadpoles or a salamander. A month or so later, the redwing blackbirds raise their families in the bullrushes. Because our house is so close to the nursery, we are among the first to hear the redwings when April snow is still on the ground. Shortly after come the killdeers, who also nest near the Frog Pond, although I think they lose most of their chicks to our cats and their feline friends.

Because there is more life there, I spend more time at the Frog Pond in the spring than I do at the larger pond in the meadow. The water in the larger pond is about neck high at its one deepest spot; the rest is about waist or knee-deep. I have caught salamand-ers there because they are easier to spot in the open water than they are in the Frog Pond's rushes, and once, in the deepest part, I saw a snapping turtle with a shell about a foot long snoozing on the dark bottom. The pond in the meadow is less than a half-acre large, and I knew it could not support the appetite of so large a carnivorous turtle. I suppose the awesome creature was there for a rest on an egg-laying journey or some sort of snapping turtle migration. I never saw it after that one spring day.

When the summer lighthouse is lit by the neighbors, I do not visit the meadow pond. I don't want to impose, and besides, I see the pond most often when I'm headed down our dirt road on the way to the bay.

After the lighthouse has been taken down and put in the neighbors' big white barn to wait for another vacation, I start paying more attention to the pond in the meadow. Through the autumn days, I check the water level, the growth of the bullrushes at the southeast end. My trips become almost daily when November arrives and the freezing nights come to Maine. I am waiting for the pond in the meadow to freeze enough so we can skate on it.

Skiers here may not like snowless Decembers; but for us pond skaters, dry Decembers are a blessing beyond measure. The first ice, almost always black and smooth, grows more perfect for skating with each cloudless and chilling night. And each December weekend that goes by without snow means that we can have one more Saturday and Sunday of skating without having to shovel first, or watching a wet snow turn the ice to crusty slush.

I work my tail off to keep that pond shoveled smooth but almost always the changing winter weather puts an end to smooth ice, no matter how persistently I shovel. When I have to admit defeat, I leave the pond until early spring. But on these December days, I skate. I can see the grass of summer still waving under the clear ice; and I hear Sam laughing as he falls and his small body slides across the new ice into the brown sedge on the bank.

This first December Saturday we skated until after sunset. Near dusk two jets flew high over us, and I wondered if the pilots could see us and all the ponds like ours, because I was hoping as we skated there alone that there are not too many people in this world without a pond, or a stream, or even a roadside ditch that fills during spring and autumn.

In the routine of my present life, my days seldom start before the sun. But lately, on several of these winter mornings, I've had to get out of bed at 5:30 to get Sam to his PeeWee hockey games. Because there is such a demand for the ice at the Bowdoin Arena, the first games start at 6:30 a.m. — a strange hour to find boys roaring around the rink, yelling, passing the puck and checking each other into the boards.

But outside our house, there is quiet. Each time I step outdoors into the dawn, leaving everyone else asleep in the still house but Sam — who is already in the car, impatient — I think of my dawns past and I am grateful for having a reason strong enough to pull me from under the covers in time to see the sun rise.

As a boy, I saw my first outdoor dawns as a hunter of ducks. Those early mornings on the water became one of the strongest influences on my life's direction. I was always happy to be in the country instead of the city where my family lived for all but a few weeks in the summer. Somehow, I managed to hitch a ride or something to the country place, much emptier then than it had been in the vacation season. With my brother Chick, or friends, I would sleep in chilly, unheated summer homes, get up much earlier than necessary, cook my own breakfast and get out on a point, or in a blind by the bay long before the eastern sky began to lighten.

When the sun rose in those times, it was a sun that illuminated the wings of black duck, that shimmered behind wavering lines of scoters, low on the water, or blinded me as I watched a flight of brant move across the sky. In my boy years, those were the most soaring times of my life. I was never more fulfilled, more at peace with myself and the world; and it was the intensity of that recognition that later led me from the city back to the country — the one place where I had found a kind of contentment.

My boyhood ended aboard the bombers I flew on during the war; yet, again, it was the dawns of those days I remember best. On the days we flew our missions, we would be awakened at two or three in the morning. Our take-off would be made in the darkness before dawn, and then, as the upper sky changed from night to day, we would circle in the big planes, high over England, joining the others in our group, arranging the separate squadrons into the tightly patterned formations we had to assume before we left friendly territory. The process was called forming; it took more than an hour, and the sun rose as we circled in and above the clouds. Being above the dawns that way made them quite different, often eerie and always dramatic. The sky would be filled with reds, greys and yellows as cloud banks became the only reference points in a surreal skyscape — a boundless and infinite place in which our screaming machines were harsh intruders, soon forgotten.

In the fear that I found in those dawns, I would seek out memories of my earlier days and think of ducks instead of bullets and plan the hunting I would do when I got back home. And I did that hunting, prone on the beach at Cedar Point, wearing the same sheepskin flight suit that had kept me warm in the stratosphere, waiting on the point before dawn for pass shooting at the whistlers, old squaw and scoters that went tearing by. It wasn't the same as it had been before; but I had to do it because I had told myself that I would.

Going back to Bonac' for the gunning became more important than carrying out a self-made promise, however. Because I was so stubborn about taking those dawns at Cedar Point, I got to know the people whom I would turn to a few years later when I almost lost myself in the city. For when those wretched urban days reached their deepest gloom, I came back to the country and began work as a fisherman with some of the men I had met as duck hunters.

As a fisherman, I saw dawns a plenty — just about every one every day for seven years. The ones I remember best are the ones I saw from the beach, when we were haul seining for bass. The crew would meet at Ted's house, sometime between 4 and 4:30, when the sky was still an absolute black. We had our breakfast snack: instant coffee and toast with peanut butter. Then, shuffling in our rubber waders, pulling on gloves and hats against the autumn cold, we would leave for the beach in the noisy trucks, pulling the net-laden dory on a trailer.

If no one had been late and the trucks had started properly, we would get to the beach just as the very palest light moved into the eastern horizon on the rim of the dark ocean. The dory would be backed down to the surf's edge, unloaded, and we would hold it there in the wash of the waves, waiting for Ted to tell us when to go. I rowed the bow oars, and held the bow steady as I waited, standing in water up to my knees, feeling the dory surge with the seas running under her. Ted would have to wait for the dawn, so he could see swells far enough offshore to pick a time when we could launch safely. Then he would say, "Get in, Jawnny," and I would climb over the gunwale, pick up my oars and brace my feet, ready to row. Sometimes a wave would break over the bow and slap me across the shoulders, surprising and chilling me; but most often Ted would pick the right time, wait a bit, tell Jim to get in and then yell to us both to row hard as he pushed the heavy boat through the seas to start us on the most critical part of our set. Jim and I would bend our backs and our oars, straining with every ounce, pulling for our survival there in those ocean dawns between the breaking waves. That's some way to start a day, I'll tell you.

Every time, if there was no trouble, we would have that first set hauled in just as the rim of the sun flared over the far sea. By the time the whole sun rested on the horizon, red and shimmering on the waves, we'd have the bunt ashore and could tell if we'd caught enough fish for a day's pay.

Nowadays, except when Sam plays hockey, I'm still in bed when some of those same fishermen are finishing that first set. But I always think of them with love whenever I get up at dawn and see the dawns of my life go by.

WILDLIFE

If I ever dream of another place to be (besides Maine), I put myself in the Carribean or some equally tropical, watery environment. The reason is not because I want the sun, although some
Maine springs have made me long for it, but because I want to
spend my days looking at fish. I'm certain my fixation for fish-
watching is fairly unique. On those few times when I have been
blessed with the opportunity to really see fish. I've become rather
painfully aware that my companions of the moment, no matter
who, failed to share my ecstasy. Like most persons who find an
unexpected and severe eccentricity in a man they thought they
knew, my fish-watching witnesses have always avoided mentioning
the episode, either while it happened or at any later date.

After some decades of such studied disinterest, I don't let it
bother me one bit and proceed with all the fish-watching I can get
whenever and wherever the occasion arises, no matter who is
startled. I'm sure many would-be-fish-watchers consider me ec-
centric simply because they are ignorant of what to watch for.
The New London ferry, for example, which travels from Connecticut to Long Island (N. Y.) is a fine fish-watcher's platform. During
a typical summer crossing I have seen mackerel, menhaden, bluefish, sand eels and shark. And, while waiting for a late ferry last
September, Marshall and I watched from the pier for at least a
half-hour while a half-dozen snapper blues deviled a school of
small herring.

That was a remarkable bit of natural drama; and now that I
recall it, one of the finest onshore fish-watching scenes of my
career. Marshall, being my trusting son, saw nothing odd in my
behavior and seemed to be as awed by the sight as I. Other waiting
passengers, however, averted their gazes from the strange two-
some who pointed at the water, stared and shouted. But the others
couldn't see what we saw.

Sheltered from the wind by the ferry slip pilings, clear with the flood tide from the sea, and lucid in the bright light of a cloudless September sun, that particular patch of water was as transparent as a crystal goblet. Below the surface, a large, silvery ball rolled erratically about in an uneven circle, starting at one corner of the slip, moving to the other side, and then back again. The "ball" was a school of thousands of sardine-sized herring, packed together as tightly as they could get, huddled in the classic protective formation of a threatened population—determined somehow to find safety in numbers.

As we watched, we could see darker and larger shapes moving slowly below the quivering, shivering, silvering orb. Whenever one fragment of the ball splintered off in a single, shining sliver, the dark shape below would become a bright rocket as the snapper blue flashed his white belly, tore upward into the herring, and— more often than not—left with the tiny straggler in his teeth.

Snapper blues are not much larger than a man's hand; and herring no longer than a little finger. Out of their element, snappers have no particular grace (except for the bluefish lover), but there under the surface of a miraculously clear patch of dirty New London harbor, the little fish were revealed as the hurtling, tearing, menacing and somehow fascinating bits of life they truly are. Because we were fish-watchers, Marsh and I spent a wonderful half-hour waiting for a late ferry that had everyone else churning with impatience.

It is no exaggeration for me to say that fish-watching has given me my most memorable outdoor moments. There was the squally afternoon one October when I watched a school of porpoise drive hordes of striped bass into the surf, and the porpoise leapt from the waves with red bass blood streaking the white porpoise bellies. Or the time a school of whales made love and frolicked in the shadow of our boat on a windy, North Atlantic afternoon in November....Such are the rewards of a fish watcher, and I could go on and on.

I think of the Carribean, you see, because the water there is still clear and full of fish; and I think of it more now than other times because if it weren't for what man has done to Maine rivers, on these May days I could watch fish from my office window that looks out over the Androscoggin River. Before it was suffocated, this river and these falls that lie at our office doorstep were among the finest fish-gathering grounds in Maine. Salmon, shad, herring, sturgeon and more could be seen from this very spot every May.

But no matter how much is done now to save the river, the fish won't return—not in my time. Which is why, as a fish-watcher, I sometimes yearn for tropic waters.

Fishing, with rod, reel, "pole", string, hook or bent pin, is the number one national American male pastime. Some call it sport, others label it recreational activity, and the people who make fishing equipment say it's big business. I like the word pastime better because it accurately indicates the rather leisurely pace fishing often acquires. Some of my finest fishing trips have been those whose hours were marked by a prolonged absence of fish, but plenty of meditation on the state of nature and the world.

On other trips there has been frantic and trembling activity when fish suddenly appeared, filling my world with the unexpected excitement of their turbulent presence. I have discovered no other moments in my life more consistently supercharged than those having to do with the surprise surfacing of vast and thrashing schools of fish. Whenever the fresh autumn winds flash out of the northwest, I can see Montauk light, North Bar, and the green slopes of the Atlantic being rent by hundreds of thousands of fish. In October there are those electric days when the air is charged with the vitality of the autumnal equinox — dry, cool, breezy and crackling with the energy of seasonal change.

The elemental phenomena does something to the fish. When the northwest wind chops at the water, the vast migratory schools flowing slowly southward like a submerged river suddenly rush to the surface in a frenzied outburst so shattering that it seems as if the fish are tearing at the very fabric of natural order. The fishermen say the water is "feather white" with the agitation of the surging fish. It is a good phrase to catch the way the leaping projectiles stir the water to foam which is caught in the wind like the feathers of a million snow white birds. And often there are birds there by the thousands. They are the terns, screaming in seeming panic and hysteria as the feeding fish leave acres of water spread with the drifting fragments of the small fish that have been decimated by the churning schools.

There are several kinds of fish that can create these awesome scenes; schools of tuna, with each fish weighing more than a hundred pounds, can rip the open Atlantic with a suddenness that thumps even the most experienced guide; striped bass, normally a fairly placid sort, can find fuel enough in the autumnal climate to become violent and visible; but it is the bluefish that has the capacity for the most incredible explosions.

The most voracious nomad of the world seas, the bluefish *(Pomatomus salatrix)* travels from New England waters to the Indian Ocean, and no man has yet recorded the erratic migrations with any degree of accuracy and predictability. But for decades now the bluefish has spent summers in the inshore waters south of Cape Cod. It is the hapless herring that brings the big blues, and the silver schools of herring change to great bloody seamarks of slaughter as the bluefish rip through the terrorized knots of defenseless mites.

The jarring vibrations of a hundred powerboats does not break the bluefish pattern of violence. I have taken my boat through the red center of a feeding frenzy and seen 15-pound blues slap the wooden hull as they hurled themselves from the water almost as if they were gripped by an uncontrollable urge to take flight, to leave their element, to become something beyond mere sea creatures. During those pressurized moments, the fish will strike at any kind of lure, and their frenzy becomes the fisherman's frenzy too. Hands bleed from clumsy contact with barbed hooks; wire leaders cut into brine soaked skin; and some fishermen have become so heedless of razor bluefish teeth that fingers have been severed, the human blood spilling into the sea to join that of the herring.

Often the frenzy can last for more than an hour. Then in the moment of some invisible sea turn, the violence ends. Exhaustion is everywhere. The fish that have been boated die as soon as they leave the water, their hearts burst with their ecstasy. The terns drift to their lonely and private shores to sit huddled and silent. The boats and fishermen move toward the harbor, the momentum of their excitement dwindling slowly with the day.

I have gone back twice to see the bluefish since I have been in Maine, for they have never come this far north. Last week, however, on a still evening in Casco Bay, the water began to roil as I fished for stripers. In ten minutes I had hooked two bluefish and discovered myself shaking with the old excitement. If my surprise catch was a signal of more bluefish on the way, you will understand my response. There are no moments more supercharged than those the bluefish can bring.

If I seem a bit preoccupied these days, you must forgive me. I have a most important appointment with *Roccus saxatilis*, and I am so afraid of being late that most of my thoughts pivot on the anticipated meeting, leaving me unable to do little else but think about what I'll do when contact is finally made. *Roccus* is perhaps my oldest and most important friend; I haven't seen him for almost a year and his arrival is always cause for great rejoicing even though we have been meeting each other this way since the 1940's.

Roccus is the generic name for the striped bass, the noblest tidewater fish of them all and for me the most symbolic of all the planet's creatures. This particular fish and myself have had a most important relationship for thirty years, and I would hope it will continue as long as I live...*Roccus* must go on forever.

The striper is a migratory creature, moving south to the Chesapeake and its environs for the winter, then trending north along the Atlantic coast as far as Newfoundland in the summer. It is a creature of the surf, the meeting place of sea and land where it is master of tumbling currents and white-water turbulence that would dizzy other fish. I have always found that meeting place the most exciting of locations and have never wanted to be far from the sea's edge. Which is how I met *Roccus*. Each of us somehow feels suffocated when we are not at the brink of the sea — I moving in from the land, and the bass swimming in from the waves.

We met first in the rolling surf of the open Atlantic along Long Island's beaches. I chose to be a fisherman because it was the only occupation that gave me honest cause to stay in the surf for most of the year. And that surf's major harvest was the striped bass — a crop I helped harvest not because I wanted to be in the business of killing fish, but because the hunt for those fish made it possible for me to know the daily exhilaration of living each day under the waves' curl. It was *Roccus,* and he alone, who made that exhilaration possible, and for that I have always loved the fish beyond most other living creatures, man or animal.

If such an analysis had to be made, I would say that I owe my life to the striped bass. Because not until I became a dory fisherman did I find the strength to live. Until then I had an existence; ever after I have had a life. The discovery of myself in the sea is what drew me to it from then on. And the appearance of the striped bass as the champion of the sea's edge gave me a natural hero to worship without reservation. Ever since those days of discovery I have been determined to live within sight of both the sea and the stripers.

Their determination was put to a frightening test when I came to Maine fourteen years ago. I had been told by fishermen that the bass annually came as far north as the waters of the state's southern coast, but I had never been here so I could not be certain. I did not have to stay uncertain long. I arrived in March, and saw striped bass in June, playing in the surf at the mouth of the Mousam River in Kennebunk. I knew then that I could stay in Maine; that I probably would never leave.

I watch fish the way a religious zealot goes to church, or a compulsive gambler buys two-dollar tickets. Each of them in their own way finds fulfillment and surcease in prayer, or playing the horses; I find mine in fish-watching, and of all the fish to watch, the bass is best.

They move singly, or in schools. They can weigh sixty pounds or one; they thrash, feed and play by day and by night; and I have been in a small boat under a full moon when the waters around me were made noisy by the opening mouths of bass as they surged to the surface after shrimp. I have seen a large bass undulate by me as I stood waist deep in a clear tidal stream while the great fish moved unafraid, almost within my reach, toward the open sea. Bass show their broad tails, waving like a mermaid's above the surface when they dive. Their dorsals often cut the surface of shoal water the way a periscope might, leaving an ever-so-slim wake feathering the wavelets. And when a school is in a feeding frenzy, the white water tossed by rolling stripers has wet me as I watched from a boat rowed carefully to the school's edge.

This morning, before breakfast, I went to the bay's brink, hoping to keep my appointment. *Roccus* was there, but we did not meet. He was too distant for me to reach, but I saw at least two, quite small bass flip out of the water; and further off shore a feeding school drew a flock of gulls for a brief while. I will go back again this afternoon and evening for another try.

Because even though I love the creature, I still fish for it. I have not successfully rationalized this seeming dilemma, nor do I torment myself with rationalizations. I love the fish, and I find it exciting to hook one on rod and reel. I use light tackle, and I release all but a half-dozen bass each season. But I do not consider our meeting complete unless I land at least one, and that is the appointment I now anticipate.

Like all important relationships, the one of I and *Roccus* is complex. I am quite certain it can never be understood by anyone but us. The way I explain it most often is by acknowledging that I used to be a bass. At that point, everyone is convinced I'm crazy.

I have to talk a bit about the eels.

I shouldn't, for a number of reasons. But perhaps the most important is the fisherman's reason for not talking about what he is doing, specifically, that is. Ambiguity is a professional fisherman's trademark. Ask a lobsterman what kind of a year he is having, and you will get an ambiguous answer, slanted toward the negative. Ask a herring seiner, a scalloper, a clam digger, a dragger or a halibut specialist what kind of a season they are having and — if they are professionals — you will get the same kind of courteous non-statement you got from the lobsterman. You can take the same answer you got ten years ago from one fisherman and tack it to all the questions about fishing you will ask a professional fisherman for the next two decades, or two centuries if you live that long. The non-answers won't change. It's a mark of the profession, like a doctor's stethoscope or an engineer's hard pencil.

So my wanting to talk about the eels is definitely non-professional — which, I suppose, has always been my trouble with fishing. I have never been quite able to contain my enthusiasm about it. Not for myself or for those around me. I can remember the first time I allowed fishing to sweep me away to another world from which I have never quite returned. If I had been able then to see the incident as objectively as I do now, I would have recognized the huge monkey already on my back. But I didn't have the perspective then. After all, I was only fourteen or so.

It was certainly one of my first formal summer dances. I can remember the burning self-consciousness and real embarrassment with which I made my entrance in my first dinner jacket. My cheeks flamed, my anger was awesome and I twisted with gangling discomfort at being thus costumed just to please my parents and the daughters of their friends ... each of the emotions combined to make me miserable with myself and the world of music, dancing (fox trot) and bouffant evening dresses that seemed to block every escape route I tried.

All but one. The dance was being held in a kind of rustic club built almost at the water's edge of Gardiner's Bay in Long Island Sound. Once I found the door to the sun deck that hung on the edge of the bay, I found myself just two steps up from the sand and the dark sanctuary of a night-time beach. I left the dance. I left with a rush of relief and purpose, almost running along the water's edge. I saw a light a half-mile or so down the beach, and I knew I was going to walk until I learned what was happening out there in the soft blackness of a summer night.

It was three or four fishermen making a set with a fairly large bay seine. They had just set the nearly half-mile of net in a half-moon curve from one spot on the beach, out into the bay, and back into shore further up the beach. The twine curtain stretched offshore in a semicircle around whatever fish were going to be caught as the fishermen at both ends of the net slowly pulled their ends ashore and shrank the half-circle a foot at a time.

By the time 600 yards of net was on the beach, the semicircle had shrunk to one just a few frantic feet across, and the fish trapped in the disappearing bit of water were beginning to thrash and churn. I had never been so excited before. I had watched the net being hauled for more than half an hour. I had listened to the fishermen's non-committal instructions and chatter, and until the net was nearly ashore, I had no idea whatsoever that they would pull all this shimmering silver from the sea. The moon washed in the turbulence of the trapped fish, the fishermen became openly excited, there were shouts, the stamping of booted feet, and then, suddenly, the entire net was ashore and the bunt quivered and trembled with perhaps three hundred pounds of weakfish for the New York market.

By that time I was in the water up to the knees of my new monkey suit, helping the men pull their catch to high ground, hanking out the net, helping to load it in the boat, doing anything I could to be noticed by the fishermen. They said nothing about my clothes, or about my help. But when the net was loaded, the fish picked up and the boat ready to be beached for the night, the crew captain said I could take a "few fish to eat."

I stuffed two in each pocket of my formal pants, and, with their tails hanging out, went back to the party. I was no longer sought after by dance minded females. More important, I had found my goal in life. I knew I had to be a fisherman.

That's how come, after twenty years in the newspaper business, I am still fishing, commercially that is. That's why I have to talk about the eels. But, you see, I'm a bit closer to being a professional, because you don't know anymore about my eel trapping now than you did when I started.

That's the way it is with all us fishermen when we talk about how we're doing.

The fog, rain and drizzle that filled the final four days of last week surely caused inconvenience, delay and possible vacation disaster to many Maine visitors, but the wet weather saved the tuna and, I think, the tuna tournament. Organizers of the annual Casco Bay tuna harpooning contest might disagree with me. They may consider their efforts severely hurt by the fog which kept the tuna boats in Mackerel Cove the final three days of the tournament. But, and I think some reflection may change their minds, I for one was grateful for the fog, and for the sanctuary it gave the giant fish.

Fifty-seven of the giants (only two weighed less than five hundred pounds) were killed the first two tournament days. That's something of a record for the affair, which has been in existence for many years. Given the same weather for the following three days, and taking into account the extra number of boats that would have turned out for the weekend, nearly one hundred more tuna could have been dead by Saturday. They were not. They were saved by the rain and the fog.

I think the tournament was saved too, because I think the killing of 150 giant tuna would have been termed a slaughter by the conservation-conscious people of the Maine coast. And a slaughter it would have been. Questions would have been asked about the purpose of such killing, a controversy would have begun, the tournament would have been clouded by dark headlines, and photographs of tuna carcasses piled on the dock at Bailey's Island might even have made the national press and been equated with photographs of the seal clubbings on the Arctic islands, or partridge kills on the hunting grounds of European royalty.

Such notoriety is always the penalty for man's excessive destruction of animals. It is a phenomenon full of ironies and touches of the absurd; it is also a phenomenon which nature seems to have a way of preventing whenever nature is given half a chance.

There are several reasons why men allow themselves to commit such excesses, but at the heart of the matter is man's frustration at being outwitted by animals. I remember my first overkill very well; its images have never left my mind, even though they were planted there on a December night thirty years ago. My brother, myself, and two of our fellow teen-agers had been duck hunting on the eastern end of Long Island (N.Y.) for three days. The weather had been the coldest in a decade, with two nights of 15° below. The bays were frozen, the ponds were closed, the shooting was terrible. Not only that, but our suffering from the cold had been considerable. Feet, faces and hands had been frostbitten, and my brother had nearly frozen to death when he fell through an air pocket in the bay ice and got soaked.

On our last day, we found an open spring at the end of a row of potato fields which bordered a large, salt bay. The open water was no more than thirty feet across—really just a puddle. But with everything else frozen tight, we knew the migrating ducks would be desperate to get to it. We came back that evening at sunset, when the black ducks moved in off the open sea. The moon was full, almost as bright as day on the snow covered fields, and the ducks swarmed over us the way moths swarm around a light. They did not fly off when we shot, and we fired until our gun barrels got too hot to hold, even in that freezing weather.

We could not carry all the ducks we had killed.

Other excesses have followed that one, but none more vivid or more guilt laden. After five years of fishing the open Atlantic surf, our haul seine came in one morning glutted with huge striped bass. It was a time we had all worked for and talked about, but the sight of those hundreds of dead fish stacked on the beach was far different from the anticipation of their catching.

It is the anticipation and the hunt that puts men in contest with animals; and it is the normal difficulty of hunting that maintains the anticipation. When nature alters conditions just enough to upset the balance, the hunt becomes ridiculously simple for the hunters, and even giant tuna can become as easy to pick from Casco Bay as hunks of floating cordwood. This probably happens once in a generation, and the men there to see it happen are most often the men who have hunted tuna for a generation. With their skills, they can take fifty-seven tuna in two days, knowing as they do that this is more tuna than they are likely to see in a lifetime. And knowing, I'm certain, some sense of regret that the huge, beautiful fish are letting themselves be killed so easily.

I have seen the tuna schooling in the bay's crystal green. I have seen the half-ton giants playing in their water like children in a room, frolicking in ponderous grace, standing on their heads and tails, rolling and sunning, turning in a kind of incredible underwater slow motion as the boat and the harpooner closed on them. There is total excitement in the contest between man and these wild and powerful fish.

But the death of fifty-seven giants in two days is an excess, which is why I was grateful for the fog which moved over Casco Bay and held the tuna boats at their docks. I'm certain some of the tuna men were grateful too.

This is the weekend the ospreys will arrive. Their coming has always been one of the bird marks of my springs, like the first March call of wild geese overhead, or the trill of the redwing, here to claim his marsh.

But I don't expect to see the osprey come to Maine; the big fish hawks are now too rare. They were not so scarce in the time and place of my growing years, spent in a house on a lake a hundred miles or so to the south. That lake, which bordered the lawn of our home just a few feet from the back porch, was kept from meeting the Atlantic Ocean by a narrow strip of sand beach a bit to the west of where I lived. The Gut was the name of the place where beach, ocean and lake came together, and almost every year the storms of early spring would raise the lake's water level so it would spill over the beach. The flooding waters gouged a channel in the shifting sands so both ocean brine and the lake's fresh water could meet in a turbulent and fertile mixing.

Alewives, those silvery fish of the herring family, migrated up that part of the Atlantic coast just about the time the Gut opened. Driven to fresh water by the deepest of their reproductive instincts, thousands of the foot-long fish would struggle across the barrier beach, against the lake's outflow until they reached the calm waters of the inner lake. While they were there, participating in their spawning ritual, the high waters would subside and the sand beach would act on its own — almost overnight — to restore itself as the legitimate barrier between lake and sea. Returning to the channel they had entered, the alewives would find they had been trapped. Nature had locked them into the lake for the summer, until they could be freed by September's equinoxial storms.

The presence of the bright fish in a wide and shallow pond was the presence that brought the ospreys. They came by the score.

One April day I counted more than forty, all fishing over that lake. It was a spring sight so common that I never appreciated the singularity of the hunt enacted for me hundreds of times a day. Yet now I realize it is a hunt never to be seen again on the scale that I saw it, and perhaps, in a few years, never to be seen again on any scale.

At the beginning of the third week in March, the twenty-first day, if I looked carefully all day, I could find the first osprey looking over the lake. In three weeks, the first would be joined by dozens, and by May there would be scores. The birds would fly in from the east, where their island rookery lay. They would arrive when the sun got well up in the sky so there would be enough light for them to see the silver fish darting under the still surface of the clear lake. Hovering on their arms-length wings, beating their dark, steely brown feathers in the wind, hanging like quivering stars in the sky, the ospreys would wait for a quarter of an hour or more for the surfacing of the alewives they were watching. Then, folding back their wings, the birds would drop in breathtaking dive, slam into the water in a frenzied white splash, extending their hooked talons as they hit. There would be a moment of stillness as the great birds recovered from their fall. If the hunt was successful, I could hear the osprey wings beating the water as the bird struggled to rise, clutching the fish in its feet.

I never tired of osprey watching; one day I saw a big male make a dive on too great a fish. The beating of the wings lasted for longer than it should, and still the bird was not airborne. His talons were locked into the fish, and, as I watched, the thrashing bird was pulled under, and there was nothing on the water to mark his going.

Thousands of ospreys have vanished since then, but they have been obliterated by the whim of man, not the laws of nature. Pesticides like DDT, as man has learned too late, build up in food chains in a way that puts the greatest concentration of residual poisons into the gullets of the fish-eating birds. Sterilized and sickened by man's chemicals, the osprey's population has faltered and slumped to the point where some scientists say the birds are now doomed to extinction. I hope not, because even though they are scarce, I still watch for them at this time of the year, and listen for their screaming call.

I saw an old and empty osprey nest last weekend on Stone Island, off Machiasport where there is talk of building an oil terminal, and I wondered if the coast of Maine may not be close to the fate of the big birds I so took for granted when they fished that lake in front of my old home.

The chickadees haven't shown up at the kitchen window, and I'm beginning to get worried. I'm definitely not a bird-watcher's man; my identification is sloppy, there are some birds I don't really care about (the complex sparrow family, for example) and I'll walk right by a warbler if I can find a plover instead. But I do enjoy seeing bird movement, bird color and bird flight in our front yard. The presence of these bright bits of life is a sprightly antidote to the insistent chill of Maine winters. Sitting at breakfast looking out at a snowscape animated by jays, chickadees, grosbeaks and a nuthatch or two makes me feel regal, as if I were one of those French kings with his own private aviary, gathered from the earth's far corners for my amusement.

Instead of sending couriers with cages to bring in my birds, I've always been able to get by with a chunk of suet, some sunflower seed, maybe a bit of millett, cracked corn and peanut butter. The combination has never failed for the last several years. Dumped into a variety of feeders (which seldom last more than a single winter) the free food has bribed all manner of birds to entertain and reassure us that life goes on, snow or no.

I became accustomed to opening the front door on my way out and looking a chickadee right in the eye as he sat stripping the hull from a sunflower seed just a few inches away. The spunky little birds are amazingly courageous and friendly. I could have touched them numbers of times, and regard them with affection. I felt bitterly betrayed when our cat would take advantage of a chickadee's neighborly innocence and make a meal of the tiny bird.

The chickadees also managed to add weather forecasting to their long list of virtues. From several years of watching their behavior at the feeder I learned to recognize their frantic, pre-storm feeding. When the chickadee crowds become noisy, fool-hardy and frenzied late on a winter afternoon, it was almost always a certain sign that snow would fall before morning. The birds sensed the coming threat to their survival and tried to store up as much fuel as possible.

This year it looks as if I have lost my feathered friends and fore-casters. The feeder has been in its place for some weeks now, and chickadee number one has yet to show. I don't have any explan-ation, except to keep telling myself that the autumn has been so fine that the birds are still in the woods and meadows, making their meals on fresh natural seeds and bugs instead of helping them-selves to a steady diet of stale sunflower seeds and cold suet. Once and awhile in the morning if I'm depressed I get dark thoughts about topics like *Silent Spring* and begin to wonder if some chem-ical disaster has overtaken the area's chickadees; but I'm not ready yet to let the idea grow. It would be too shattering, too destruc-tive to the philosophical sustenance of my winter.

Besides, other birds have survived: namely, the bluejays. They shove at each other most mornings, screeching and stuffing their considerable faces with as many seeds as their gizzards can hold. Like squirrels, the bluejays seem to have a tendency to store up for the winter; I can't imagine that they eat all the bulk they carry away. I'm sure there is a vast deposit of sunflower seeds in some hollow tree that I'll find years from now.

But as much as I welcome the jays and their arrogant good looks, I would gladly trade them all for one chickadee, nuthatch or junco. I haven't gone to all the trouble (and I'm the one who does it) of filling the feeders, getting the suet, and making certain my breakfast seat is the one closest to the window just so I can watch a bunch of jays scrap over who gets how much first. Even the cats won't mess around when the bluejays take over.

Nor do I relish the prospect of facing a February or March with only the jay's screech as background music. There is something much more reassuring in the "chickadee-dee-dee" that the black caps repeat with such insistent vigor, even though the wind may be howling from the northeast and freezing rain is slatting over the roof. The sound of the chickadee is instant courage for any man, wearied by March, worried by the weather. The sight of the small grey bird, talking it all away as he sits with feathers puffed against the cold is a sight of ultimate reassurance. Without it, I can visualize the entire household losing the will to go on.

And on top of this, I say to myself, how can I ever explain the absence of the official state bird from the feeder of the editor of Maine's only statewide journal of opinion? I mean, what kind of environmentalist nature freak can't commune with a chickadee?

The questions become even more ominous when they're coupled with a bit of distressing information I got handed just the other day. I was talking about the chickadee absence with a neighbor, who promptly told me nothing serious could be wrong because his yard was crammed with the birds; indeed (he rubbed it in) they had been there all summer. That is precisely the sort of information I can not live with easily. If the chickadees don't show up at our house soon, I'm going to issue an official call for help.

The wind was blowing from the east when I got home, and when I got out of the car I could hear the black ducks talking together in the marshy cove about three-quarters of a mile from the house. The place is about due west of the cove, so when the wind is easterly, or there is no wind at all, I can hear the wild water bird sounds—the talking, the calling, the splashing and the slapping of wings on the water. The sounds always delight me. They remind me of times when I hunted ducks and listened excitedly all night long to their talking, only to find them gone by dawn; or other times here in Maine when the sound of a calling goose meant that the ice had left the bay and winter would ease.

My homecoming salutation was the first I had heard this fall, and because of this it was a double delight. I had grown anxious about the absence of the birds and hoped that some ecological change had not forced them to alter their travel patterns and skip their stops at the upper end of Middle Bay. As I stood listening in the wet wind, responding to my visitors with my own duck talk (which they answered) I realized that I was the only person at home. It was the silence of the empty house, as much as the easterly breeze, which allowed me to hear the black ducks.

It was the noise of the homestead, I decided, which had kept me from hearing any water birds earlier this fall. That night last week was the first time in months I had arrived home and found it deserted. The ponies were out in the field, and whinnied to be taken to their stalls and fed; the cats were underfoot, wanting in out of the drizzle, four kittens were romping in the barn, and two of the four dogs hadn't made it to the car in time for the shopping errand, or whatever it was that had taken the younger children and their mother downtown. Aside from a whinny or two, there was absolute silence. The driveway was empty of cars and, most notable, there was not a sound coming from the boys' room.

Which was why the silence was so absolute. The little people and the lady of the house have often been away at the evening time when I reach home. They are busy too, and seem to have an endless round of after-school activities which require all manner of special trips in the late afternoon. But one of the four boys is always home, and when they are they always have their record player playing—loud. This means that on my quieter homecomings, I am greeted by the sound of rock, folk, jazz or soul, depending on which of the boys commands the turntable. If the little people arc also on hand, the amplified music is joined by shrill calls, the barking of dogs and the background confusion of whatever television show the kids are not watching.

But on this night, I was alone. An incredible combination of simultaneous but independent interests had removed the four boys from under their roof. The silence and the solitude were a luxury I began to savor more and more as I realized why I was hearing the black ducks so clearly.

It might be different if silence were also a part of my work. It most definitely is not. The office is crowded, the people in it are mostly loud and noisy. The phone rings constantly; one of Maine's busiest truck routes is inches from my window; and, to top it off, the town's fire whistle perches on the roof of the nearest building. Every day at noon the whistle blows twice (as if to underscore its function) with shattering surprise; and when there's a firstclass fire, the whistle and the engine sirens together make me wish for deafness or a return to the silence of my former occupation.

As a small-time commercial fisherman, I knew silence well. It was my constant companion as I worked alone at clamming, scalloping or whatever took me out alone in my boat. Clamming had to be done at anchor, so there were no engine sounds. Scalloping was required by law to be done only under sail. Spending the hours from dawn until dusk working alone in a small boat fairly far from shore is quiet work. The slap of the sea at the boat's wooden sides, the splashing as the dredge or rake is washed, the tumbling of shells and stones onto the culling board, the cries of the terns and the gulls' harsh chatter....these and the constant sighing of the wind at my ear were the sounds and silences of my days.

Those, and my own voice. Because I would break the regularity of silence with my own irregular talk. Sometimes, if the day went well, it would be a kind of chant; other times it would be a repetition of curses, or pleadings with the scallop gods to be kind; or a kind of monologue with the clams—a discussion of their life and mine and how dependent one was upon the other.

I don't have those conversations with myself any more, not because I've gotten bored, but because there is never enough silence these days. Between a busy office and a bustling home, it is difficult to find silence enough to hear the black ducks talking in the cove, or my own voice asking if seeking more silence might not be better for us all.

Soon the falcons will be flying. They will come with the northwest winds of September, and their clean wings will ride the dry air of autumn.

I don't know if there is a precise date for the migratory flight of the falcons. There well might be. I know the ospreys have returned north each year of my life on the 21st day of March, and do so still, even though their nests and their lives have been wretchedly disfigured by man's insecticides. But I have never noticed if the falcons move on any particular September day. I know only the kind of day it will be when I first take note of their flight.

There must be the northwest wind. It comes as the messenger of a rising barometer, and its herald is a sunset which cuts the western horizon with a pale green blade, slicing through the usual smoke of dusk. After such a twilight, the dawn comes clear, cold for the season, and turning leaves rattle before sun-up in the first breezes of a nor'wester. As the sun climbs, its blazing brightness undimmed by any humid haze, the wind gathers itself for an all-day race across the fields, pushing the shadows of puffy clouds before it as it goes

Such days are not unusual in the fall and early winter; they come often and we can each recognize them as harbingers of cold. But the first of the northwest days are impressive because they mark such a change from the August fog. And they bring the falcons.

The birds, I think, wait for the wind. They are traveling southeast, and the northwest wind stream carries them along, gliding fast on the rough currents like frail canoes riding the invisible white water of airborne rapids. Look up on the first nor' west day and you will see them — sparrow hawks, pigeon hawks, Cooper's hawks, sharp-shinned hawks — birds of the hawk family accipiter, which includes such royal members as the peregrine falcon, the gyrfalcon, and other regal types whose ancestors perched on the wrists of princes and kings. Their wings are long, thin, sharp, built for speed, and their flight is flashy, none of the slow circles of the red-shouldered hawk, or the lazy gliding of the marsh hawk.

Falcons are speed. Their killing dives strike other birds in mid-flight; their plummeting stoops on grounded prey are almost too fast for man's eye to follow. Yet in September's early days, the falcons fly over us in a dashing display which you might never see if you don't feel the first northwest wind and look to the sky above. I have read somewhere, sometime, how many there are on that migratory journey. There is a mountain peak in Pennsylvania which the falcons of the northeast use as some kind of beacon on their annual autumnal voyage, and thousands of the handsome birds have been counted flashing by on the wings of the wind.

When I killed them, I counted more than a hundred falcons flying in a single northwester day. That was when I was a boy — a boy filled with excitement for guns, for bird shooting of any kind: ducks, shag, hawks, crows, plover, quail, pheasant and rail. With a friend, our shotguns and a battered stuffed owl lashed atop a long pole, I climbed a morning hilltop that overlooked the sea and waited for the birds that rode the wind. The mock owl, sitting in stupid silence and fearless immobility, was seen by the keen-eyed hawks as they sped along the rivers of the sky. Screaming their eerie, high-pitched cry, the falcons tumbled from their flight, folded their wings and dove fearlessly at the decoy and into our guns.

At the end of a morning we picked up the bodies of twenty shattered falcons—sparrow, pigeon and Cooper's hawks, the fierceness somehow still in their eyes, their nobility unrelenting even in death. And though the blood sport was much with me, and I had persuaded myself that these were birds of prey eligible for killing, I could not shake off the fierce eyes glowing from the proud heads.

I shot only one more falcon. It was that same September. The northwest wind woke me one dawn; I heard a hawk's scream and went out with my gun on the upstairs porch that bordered our room. A sparrow hawk flashed over the house; I fired and with its wings folded, the bird fell for a long time into the wooded valley below. I stayed out there until the sun rose over the water and sparkled on the wavelets scattered by a gathering wind.

I have had enough of guns. Too much, and shortly after my falcon shooting days, I was the one who was shot at in the sky. Perhaps that had something to do with the end of my time as a hawk killer. Now, in some kind of plea for their forgiveness, I watch for the birds each September and wait for the first northwest winds that will bring them. For the flashing wings tell me that in spite of my brutality, in spite of all of man's mistakes, the falcons still fly.

Correction: To keep the ornithological record straight, I must clarify an error in last week's column about the falcons in which I said that falcons are members of the hawk family accipiter. I should have rechecked my memory. The falcons are their own hawk family, and so are the accipiters, which includes the Cooper's hawk and the sharp-shinned hawk, which, then, are not quite the proper falcons I made them out to be.

One morning this winter, as I sat on the edge of the bed pulling myself from sleep and looking out the window to get a fix on the new day, I was jolted by the sight of three ringneck pheasant stepping along the road that borders our lawn. Two dun hens led by a handsome cock were making their leisurely way past the house with the kind of brave ignorance that has always been a characteristic of this odd and misplaced bird.

I was surprised and delighted. For one thing, the sight of the birds in January told me they had escaped the guns of the hunters and it pleased me that our woods and fields might have helped the strategy of survival. I have never been a supporter of the Maine sportsmen's policy which encourages the state to raise pheasant during the spring and summer so they can be "liberated" in the fall for hunters to shoot almost as soon as the birds are dropped from the state truck. Maine has the grouse as a true native bird, wily and hard to hunt. It has always seemed to me that Maine hunters who sponsor the released pheasant program are those who have neither the skill or the inclination to take a partridge or a woodcock on its own terms. Instead, they boom away at a non-Maine, hand-raised bird that has about as much intelligence and fear of man as a domestic chicken.

I know, because I used to hunt pheasant—which is another reason I was delighted to see them stroll by my home. Their procession along the road was equalled by another procession of pheasant memories which dropped like a series of flashcards across the blank screen of my early morning mind.

There were pheasant all through my boyhood. The coastal village where I spent as much of my autumns as school would allow was thick with pheasant. They could not be hunted in the inner village, and so they multiplied with astonishing fecundity and became living lawn ornaments for the hundreds of country homes on the village fringe. My springs were haunted by the sharp, metallic honkings of the cock birds as they courted their harem of hens; my summer mornings were splashed with the incredible colors of the ringneck as he strutted along the hedgerows and across the soft brown earth of plowed potato fields; and in those autumns of my teens I would bend the laws of the town by shooting a pheasant or two when they were just inside the village limits. The birds were so tasty roasted and so tempting to a young and brash hunter that I could never resist, in spite of the guilt that rolled over me when I picked up the downed bird and knew again the incredible iridescence of its intricate feathers.

When I suffered the first reaction to my rebellion in the U.S. Army, I was in Sioux Falls, South Dakota, and my educational days on the rock pile were made quite glorious by the frequent visits I would get from the pheasants of that summer. Later, in England, (my rebellion had failed) on a rest from combat on some English lord's estate, I was startled on a walk by the explosive first flight of a pheasant that rose at my feet.

It is strange that these strange birds should have gained such a foothold in my life. The ringneck is not even native to this nation, much less Maine. The bird is an Asian import, where its ancestor spawned the largest and most rugged family of birds in the world. Among others, the family includes chickens, and I think that is why I have always had doubts about the pheasant's intelligence.

It really should not be hunted; it's too dumb. It is not even quite bright enough to survive most Maine winters. Not that it should have to be, of course. Man brought the pheasant here from China; man kept trying to stretch the bird's range, and now raises the creature in pens in Maine so it can be shot in the fall, or killed by Maine's snowy winters which deny the vain pheasants the chance to find food.

But I like the birds. They are so lovely, so oriental, so arrogant, so pompous and, in a way, so delightfully comic and wild that I'm grateful they have been such a part of my life. I'll argue the pheasant's virtues with any man, and my arguments will be subjective, slanted, sentimental and totally irrefutable.

I have an affection for the birds, and the early morning sight of the trio on our road was a moment of joy. Since then I have seen the same group twice more, and have seen tracks in the snow of at least six birds. (The state truck must have gotten to our dead end road with quite a surplus.) I have had some city visitors who report putting up "a big flock" but I've never seen it.

The one positive note of this snowless winter is that it has been easy on the pheasant. I'm beginning to think now that they will survive. To help them along, Marsh and I have been watching for their tracks in new snow, and tossing a bucket or so of cracked corn in the area as a pheasant food supplement. For if the crazy birds do make it, the hens will each hatch at least a dozen eggs. If there are three hens, that means three dozen potential lawn ornaments and romantic reminders for our place. Then I'll see them at the start of my day more than once a winter; although none will equal the surprised delight of that first hello this January.

Captain's Log of a Short Sail Around Middle Bay: distance, less than five nautical miles, mostly in a circle; time, about two hours; weather, stiff sou'west breeze.

Several flocks of white-winged scoters in the bay; probably driven in by the onshore breeze which has been blowing now for at least three days. The young scoters are comical and awkward, obviously not yet sophisticated in the ways of men or boats. I remember them as "coots", as all three species of scoters were called during my gunning days in Gardiners Bay. But those ended a while ago, and here in Maine, the young whitewings are my unwitting playmates. Sailing downwind, directly at the flocks of the large sea ducks, I discover the young birds have little or no fear of the boat. Because they cannot take off, except directly into the wind, the birds are in a bit of a quandary when they comprehend how fast my Hobie Cat is closing on them. Too late they realize that if they try to take wing, they will have to fly directly into the boat. One or two try this, their wings beating the water frantically as they run—slapslapslap slap slapslap—with their crazy webbed feet pushing at the water. They are airborne within inches of the bow; I can see the whites of their eyes, their startled looks, their total discomfort and embarrassment at being caught in such a predicament. I could almost reach up and pluck one out of the air, but I laugh as they go by and spend the next half-hour or so tacking upwind of the flocks and replaying the silly game. The birds learn after a time or two, and instead of flying, they dive.

A bit weary of the breeze in the open bay and the unending demands it makes on me and the boat, I ease into a favorite small cove on the lee side of one of the half-dozen islands in my home bay. I have always loved this cove. The island is not lived on, yet some natural whim has put what amounts to a mini-meadow at the water's edge. The open green is ringed with high pines, it shelves easily to the water and is one of the most inviting spots for a small boat sailor I have ever seen. It is almost too perfect, rather like a movie set, or picture postcard. This day, I do not go ashore, but ease the boat along the shore's edge, just looking things over, enjoying the quiet and the calm of the lee.

As I glide (and this boat is a great glider) a pair of mergansers (sheldrake) slip off the shore and start paddling in front of the boat. I know these are normally open water ducks, and believe they must have a nest in the cove if they are staying here, alone, as a pair. My nesting theory seems to be upheld when the male sheldrake goes into his crippled wing act and flutters and splashes in evident distress right in front of my boat. He manages to stay a safe distance away, though, and his flutters consistently take him (and hopefully me) in a direction away from the cove. The bird is so obviously alarmed and so distinctly courageous that I do not test him any further. I sail away from the cove, and out in the open bay I come across the female sheldrake, nonchalantly paddling about, quite confident, I guess, that her male companion is doing right by the children. The fem lib movement, I decide, will never get very far with the mergansers. Their hens seem to have already won the battle, because in most other species it is the female bird that pretends to be crippled.

On the point of the island just across the channel from the sheldrake cove is a large rock that belongs to the seals. There are many other rocks in the bay, but the seals have chosen this one. They can be found there almost every day, sunning and surfing, chasing herring, mackerel and whatever. This day, there are about a dozen taking the sun. They have been out of the water for a spell, because their fur is dry and they are sleepy. They too have some young, and they don't notice my boat until it is quite near. Then there is a shuffling surge, many heads in the air, flippers pushing, big bodies sliding and slipping and splashing all about, and the rock is quite empty. By then, I am almost on top of the seals and the water is shoal. Too shoal for them to deep dive, and I can look down all around me and see the seal bodies flashing underneath.

They are curious creatures, you know, and one big fellow surfaces just next to the bow, snorting and somewhat cross at having his nap upset.

The strong breeze puffs into my sail, and I'm away before the others can surface. I sail home, imagining that someone seeing the boat from shore might think it a lonely sport to be the only boat on the bay. They couldn't have seen all my company.

Booted men, duck boats on trailers, the distant roll of hundreds of shotguns fired over Merrymeeting Bay have let me know that the duck hunting season has opened for this year. I have been something less than honest in past columns about why I no longer take part in the annual gunning. I have made myself out to be a noble non-violent type who quit killing birds because my reverence for life outweighed my hunter instincts. This is partially true; as a person whose fondest boyhood memories are of duck shooting days and as a gunner with a considerable reputation as a good shot, it took something more than just circumstance to get me to give up a sentimental and ego building pastime.

But the circumstance did play an important role, and its details are so ghastly that they have never before been revealed to anyone except the principals involved. It is time, now that the birds are flying and the guns are firing, to set the record straight, if only to ease my own conscience of the burden my overstated piety has put upon it.

It was three years ago, exactly ten hours after the opening day of that gunning season had passed, that I gave up the sport—officially and forever. My brother (sixteen months my junior) Chick, who had been one of my boyhood gunning companions, hadn't hunted with me for years. He had, however, heard me raving about the vast numbers of birds in Merrymeeting Bay, and turned up at my house late in the evening on the night before opening day. He had come to be my guest on what had been billed as the greatest gunning day of his experience—so great that for the occasion he had borrowed a very fine shotgun from a neighbor of his in Connecticut.

Even though both of us are (and were) past two-score years, we stayed up late talking because we were too excited by the prospect of the dawn. Besides, we had to leave for Merrymeeting at around three a.m., and what was the purpose of sleeping for just a few hours. So we ended up on the road for Pleasant Point at just about three, driving slowly in a white, cotton-thick and chilly autumn fog.

I successfully masked my anxiety. After all, Chick had heard nothing from me except how marvelous was my knowledge, how vast my hunting skill. Drenched by the propaganda deluge, he had no way of knowing that I didn't know my way around the bay well enough to get from Point A to Point B in the fog; I had been counting on the help of a bright moon and the prospect of following other hunters who did know where they were headed.

Along with the fog, as I learned when we reached Merrymeeting, I would have to cope with dead low tide — a condition which turns that otherwise lovely body of water into sea of black mud. But we left the dock anyway, my little outboard churning from the stern of a borrowed gunning float. As soon as we got out of range of the dock light, I was lost, sealed inside an envelope of fog. Thirty seconds later we ran aground, the motor stalled as the propellor tried to revolve in gummy ooze.

I could not get it started again, nor could we get ungrounded. We got out, slopped through the knee-deep mud in our leaky boots, grunting and cursing as we pulled the boat behind us, dragging it in sheer stubbornness across mud flats that, for all we knew, were endless.

A bit of sedge loomed up, just three feet away by the time the fog and the gloom revealed it. "This looks like a good spot," I said, terrified that if we lost sight of it we would be wandering once again. I jumped out, threw out the decoys and pulled the punt into the grass where we waited. There was no dawn or sunrise; the fog was too thick for that. The light grew around us, and we could hear ducks gabbling and flying, but we saw nothing until the fog finally lifted and we found we were established about twenty yards away from another group of hunters. They were larger and had a larger spread of decoys than we, so Chick and I picked up our rig, and he began rowing while other hunters all over the bay shot ducks. It was not a memorable moment.

When some of the other gunners were heading home, we found a spot near a point and actually began shooting at some ducks. None were hit, most were too far away, so it was understandable when Chick stood up (nearly getting his head shot off by my blast) to fire at a lone teal crossing directly overhead. The adrenalin was too much for the boy. As he fired, his gun left his hand and dropped into the now high waters of the bay. With ashen face, Chick stripped to his long johns and began diving for the prize he could not go home without.

Blue and shivering, he finally found it. When he did, I heroically managed to start the motor, and headed back for the dock with a wretched, duckless, wet and frightened brother in the bow. I was taking just a bit of pleasure, however, in the fact that the motor was running.

At least it ran until we got near the dock when I navigated directly over a submerged log that flipped my motor off the stern and into the bay. The motor has never run since, my brother has never returned to Maine, and I have never again been duck shooting.

We were waiting for a traffic light to change when a car on the other arm of the intersection drove slowly in front of us, a large, dead, black bear sprawled over the rear deck, its "arms" and legs lashed to opposite sides of the bumper. Against the white car, the bear's dark bulk was huge. I can still see it. As it went by us, I thought to myself: it could be a man. And Marsh, speaking aloud, said, "That bear looks like a person."

When the light changed, we drove ahead and had gone quite a way before Marsh spoke again. "I could never shoot an animal," he said. "I mean, not just go out in the woods to kill one. What right have we got to take their lives away, to sentence them to death, just because we have a gun and they don't?"

That hunting season for Maine is over now. More bears will be shot, of course, but now that November is gone, there won't be so many hunters in the woods. The deer season, the one that draws most of the riflemen from their living rooms, is over for this year.

Perhaps, some day sooner than any of us can imagine, it will be over for good. I have a feeling that it won't be too long before a large majority of men will decide killing wild animals is no longer necessary, either for sport or food. I say "too long" in terms of decades, which, after all, is a brief time span in relation to the five thousand years or so men have been killing in the woods.

I say this with no malice toward hunters, not as a group. There are some, like the ones who shot holes in our sign and mailbox, or who leave their litter in the woods and along the road, for whom I have negative thoughts; but for most I have a real affection and "sympatico." The good hunters are the men who understand nature, and hunt because shooting is done in the woods, under the open sky. They give the deer credit for speed and beauty, the bear's courage is acknowledged. They shoot only what they can use; they feel both pride and regret when the killing shot is fired. They are, generally, soft-spoken and quiet men.

I have been with them many times, for I have also hunted. I have never shot a deer, yet I would have had I grown up in Maine. But I have stopped shooting, and so have many of the men who hunted with me. Those who continue to hunt do it more as a ritual than a sport, and are content with one bird, or two.

I think this is happening because of a basic change in our culture, not because many of my friends are in their forties, or more. Actually, for many of them, it is easier to hunt now (they have the time and the money) than it was when they were young. They ease off of their hunting because they begin to realize that much has changed in our lifetime. Man is now working to save many of the animals he hunted fifty years ago. Man now understands that he can wipe out entire wildlife populations; while at the same time he knows he no longer needs the food he brings from the forest.

There doesn't seem to be much in a statistical way to test my observation. Hunting licenses sold in Maine are not a fair measure. There are too many immeasurable factors. Hunting pressure, for example, in neighboring states has become so intense it forces more and more men to head for Maine because there is no place left to go in their native states. Increasing affluence, the ease of

102

transportation, the growing New England population, the promotion of Maine as a hunter's paradise—all of these would have the effect of swelling the number of Maine licenses sold, even if a great many men had made a decision to do no more killing.

And it's not that these men are becoming urbanized. On the contrary, the men who quit hunting most often do it because they move philosophically closer to nature, not further away. There seems to be a strong realization by these men that the time of the hunter has come to an end. That five thousand years of survival has now created technological man, who farms all his food and hunts none. And the same technology has made man's doomsday possible, but possible only if killing is considered moral, the way a hunter considers it. Man will stop hunting, and the animals will be saved; but man will have stopped shooting because it became a threat to man.

We are in the process of this change, I think. I believe we can step outside our culture and tag it as a time in history when men began to think about hunting no longer. I think this is a good thing to happen; but I never thought hunting was a bad thing. I think it is coming to an end.

That end will change Maine in ways I can't yet anticipate; and it will change the way young Maine men and boys look at their November woods. They will have a relationship with these woods, these meadows and these waters, but it will be different from the one that I have, because I first came to know the woods as hunter. Those who come to know them only as men will have much different feelings about the community of the deer and the bear. And the bear will no longer be strapped on the backs of cars.

For a house seven miles from the hub of the Athens of Maine, ours often seems in the midst of Maine's deepest woods. It surely is if it is measured against the wildlife that shares the neighborhood. Within past recent years, I have seen (among other flora and fauna) ducks and geese of at least a dozen or fifteen different varieties; shore birds of such exotic ancestry as curlews and do-witchers, not to mention golden plover; hawks of most northeast-ern species, and of course this includes a visit from both eagle and osprey; there is a family of gun wise partridge that lives in the woods just across the road, and one spring I followed Mrs. P through the pines as she shepherded her brood of some dozen chicks carefully into the thicket as our golden retriever pup went running in the opposite direction.

The bird list could go on and on; at least once a year a small squadron (two, three or five) of snow geese fly over the barn, usually at the tailend of one of the March flocks of Canada geese. But beyond the birds are other non-human visitors of almost every sort. With a pond, marsh, salt and fresh water both almost at the doorstep, I have seen almost every sort of reptile and amphibian known to Maine. This includes frogs, toads, snakes and salamand-ers of astonishing variety, as well as turtles, seals, porpoise, striped bass, dog fish, green crab, snail and sand eel. Even a whale has surfaced on our horizon, its awesome spout showing steamy white in the cold green air of late fall.

But it's the four-footers that make life so interesting. This in-cludes the squirrels — red, grey and flying — chipmunks, deer mice, field mice, moles, shrews and a wandering rat or two that turn up around the place quite commonly, as well as the skunks, raccoons, muskrats and groundhogs that are not quite so common, but are hardly worth noting they are seen so regularly.

Beyond them are the porcupines — seen only rarely, even though their quills turn up in the dogs' noses fairly often — and the foxes, especially the Fox of the Pennellvilles. I have never seen him in daylight, only his silhouette at dusk, dark and gliding against the western sky. Yet I have heard his terrifying cry every fall for the last three. He walks along the dirt road, or in the mea-dow just beyond, and gives the fox cry. But his (or could it be hers?) is louder than any other fox any of us have ever heard. It is the shriek of every soul screaming for release from perdition; it is the cry of every murdered infant; of every damned spirit that searches the earth for forgiveness — it is a sound which no human can hear without feeling the throb of fear, without knowing that beyond this place there lies the dark void of the wandering dead.

Beyond the dark moments of the fox are the lighter thrills given us by the deer and the moose, of which I hesitate to talk because some idiot will come down here looking for them with a gun, and this is no place for guns; there are too many in other places.

There is a family of moose that still uses this place as home. They travel in a kind of circle, starting in the depths of the woods between the house and town, and including the two ponds and the fields that unfold from our home. I have seen the entire family entourage together only once: father, mother and two twin mooselets, age about six months when I saw them two years ago. The father is regal, huge and walks in stately, seven-foot strides, he is not often seen. The best view came one October morning as he strode across the length of the meadow, crossing the road just in back of the barn. He moved like a giraffe — his legs and body in motion, but his noble head and stretching rack staying calm, regal and unfrightened as he paced by the row of humans watching in awe. The cow and the twins show up from time to time, even doing things as undignified as somehow getting caught behind a fence bordering a neighbor's front lawn.

The deer are not so stupid. They are elusive, shy and delicate. I have seen them only three times, but each has been the more memorable for it.

Just the other morning I saw, for the first time, the most determined recluse of all our visitors — the woodcock. He was in the pines, a few feet from the edge of the lawn, poking his long bill into the just thawed mud for food, and he stayed on the job even though I got quite near. I don't know about you, but for me being able to watch a woodcock get his breakfast as I'm on my way to the office — that makes a statement about living in Maine better than almost any other way I could say it. And that's why so many of my best friends are non-humans. They make the finest kind of neighbors.

There must be more deer hunters in Maine this November than ever before. I know the Fish & Game people say the total amount of licenses sold has stayed fairly level over the past few years;

but judging from what I've observed in the first half of this November, the 1970 season will go on the books as a record setter.

When it does, questions will be raised about the future of the sport in this state, and I'm already certain there will be no easy answers. In a way, the approaching discussion of deer hunting will be one more argument about the destiny of Maine.

The stage has already been set. I flipped through October issues of *Sports Afield, Field & Stream,* and several other outdoor magazines last month, and each one published a major article on deer hunting. The pattern was the same throughout: splashy illustrations glorifying the artist's version of "Superdeer"; copy which highlighted Maine as an excellent spot for hunting the whitetail; and a statement which claimed essentially that there is no more noble or challenging moment for the sportsman than the time when be brings down his buck.

There are few hunters, or would-be hunters, who can resist that kind of enticement. When you consider that there are 70 million people within a day's drive of Maine, it's a wonder more of the sportsmen among them aren't on their way. Who can blame them? They want the thrill of being in the Maine woods. They see themselves in those *Field & Stream* illustrations. They dream of driving home with a ten-point buck on the fender. As blue-collar and white-collar workers in the anonymous mass of some city, they see their moment of glory in the Maine woods as a time of reaffirmation that they are, after all, something more than time-card punchers or assembly line robots.

So they come to Maine. They are coming in such numbers that they produce stories like the one about the opening-day deer that was being hunted simultaneously by twenty-five trophy seekers, one of whom was wounded in the fusillade which brought down the doe. Or the vignette about the great buck that strode through a clearing just beyond the boundary of a game preserve. Hunters who had thought they were the only ones waiting for the buck were surprised when they stood to shoot and found themselves in the line of fire, or aiming at other hunters around the clearing's circumference. Fear of shooting each other forced them to hold their fire as the buck stepped through. The guns swung around as the trophy deer left the clearing and stepped onto the road which marked the sanctuary boundary. The hunters could have fired without hitting each other, but this time their cars parked along the roadside could have been hit. As the men hesitated about the possibility of putting a slug in their own Buicks and Oldsmobiles, the deer stepped across the road and slipped into the pines of the game preserve.

That deer found safety in the numbers of hunters who have come to Maine this month; but a grisly number of hunters have not been so lucky. As the hunting pressure increases, so do the number of hunting accidents; and the list of victims killed and wounded is still growing. So too must be the list of non-deer animals, like moose, cattle, horses and dogs—all of which have been killed in past mistakes.

It is this aspect of November which I feel the most. As non-hunters, I and my family grow anxious about the ponies when we see carloads of men in day-glo orange caps moving slowly along our roads. We fear for the large dogs like our goldens, and we are on edge about walking in our woods or meadows when we see empty cars with out-of-state plates parked along the roadside, or we hear the crack of a rifle deep in the pines.

We are relieved and happier when November is over. It is a tense time for country people. Yet I cannot resent the hunters; not really. My neighbor hunts, and hunts well. He counts on his venison to feed his family through the winter, as he always has during his long Maine lifetime. There are thousands of hunters like him in the state—men who need the meat. They are, most often, somehow quieter about their hunting than the hunting groups who drive here from across the border, but who is to say these men from out-of-state need their personal reaffirmation less than the native needs his venison.

Yet all of us know the days of free and open hunting are numbered. There will be more limitations, as there have inevitably been in other states. Townships will extend their no-hunting zones. Weapons will be restricted and high-powered rifles will be used only in wilderness areas. Out-of-state license fees may be raised; seasons may be shortened; trespass laws will be stiffened; sanctuary areas will be enlarged. Hopefully, through all this, the hunter and non-hunter won't become enemies; and hopefully, the Maine man who needs his deer to eat will continue to get it with the same quiet skill (legal and illegal) that he now employs.

The times they are a changing, and it is the change from a hunting to a non-hunting culture that is just beginning to flutter in Maine. I haven't felt the tremors until this November, but now when I see (and wave to) the men under the orange caps along the country roads, I know I'm seeing a flooding tide that will soon have to ebb. How quickly it happened. Too quickly for many older hunters to comprehend; when they were boys, there was no such thing as a deer hunting season. They hunted when they were hungry.

MORE ABOUT THE AUTHOR

I was going to write about the dead deer and bear that have been passing this office atop sedans, sprawled across fenders, or dumped soddenly into the backs of hundreds of pickup trucks, I have a new theory about the time of the hunter, the time for killing and the way it has changed my generation, and Maine. But that can wait for next week, because just as I sat down to write, I realized that it will be Thanksgiving when this column appears. We haven't taken note of the holiday elsewhere in this issue, except to get the pages to the printer early; and I'm enough of a sentimentalist to want to give an official nod to Thanksgiving on behalf of the season and those readers who might like to be nudged into recalling their own holiday memories.

One of the reasons, of course, that we look back to childhood Thanksgivings is that the holiday season holds few joys for adults. There is a pile of work to be done; a great deal of unbudgeted money must be spent; the stores get more crowded by the day, and Christmas with its frantic materialism and ever longer shopping lists is suddenly a threat instead of a bright promise.

It is therapeutic at these times to look back through the years so far that the scenes remembered have been sweetened with the sugar of time even though their reality may have been just as bitter and disturbing as any tableau that will be acted out this Thursday, I know that if I scrutinize my young Thanksgivings too sharply, I will see again all the moments of misery that dripped into the day's activities like cold rain through a leaky roof. Such moments were inevitable; they are in anyone's life, because people never act the way they look in the Norman Rockwell paintings that used to adorn the *Saturday Evening Post* covers my grandfather would bring with him as his personal reading matter while he waited for his Thanksgiving dinner.

He, himself, was close to being a Norman Rockwell all-American saint, which is perhaps one of the reasons my grandfather usually appeared with something to read. We had a formal household in those days, and Thanksgiving was always at our house on 65th Street in New York City. My grandparents (maternal) were the first to arrive, and my grandfather invariably wore his swallow-tailed morning coat, stiff shirt, striped trousers and Peale patent leather black shoes. For several years, he wore a top hat which he could collapse into a flat, black plate, and then open by tapping the brim smartly on his wrist. The hat opened with a fine "pop", and the trick was a hit with the children. I was sorry when top hats went out of style and my grandfather changed to a derby.

He and my grandmother would sit in the drawing room, rather stiffly, waiting for my mother to finish decorating the dining room. My brothers and I tried to avoid this awkward and extended waiting period, and we most often managed to do it by taking a walk to Central Park to feed the ducks at the 59th Street pond. While we were gone, my father would try to give his wife's mother as many cocktails as she could be persuaded to swallow (my grandfather didn't drink). As he plied his mother-in-law, my father also helped himself. He was usually quite cheerful by the time my Uncle Henry (also dressed to the nines) and Aunt Kas arrived, this being somewhere about 1:30 in the afternoon. My brothers and I tried to be home for Uncle Henry, because he had a delightful practice of slipping us crisp, new, five-dollar bills. And, every other Thanksgiving or so, my Uncle John, never known to refuse a drink, would roll in full of cheer.

After keeping the group waiting for more than an hour, my mother would perfect her stunning table decor and join the party. She seldom had more than one cocktail, but for her that was quite enough. By the time she led the procession to the dining room, everyone but the children and my grandfather was pretty well smashed.

The combination of gin, empty stomachs, and the awkwardness of a family group unaccustomed to prolonged conversation with each other led to some wild and woolly encounters around that lovely, long table. As we grew into our teens, it was usually my brother and myself who took the brunt. I guess we were pretty fresh kids, and we never realized how the alcohol added to the arguments of our elders. Quite often my mother would be in tears by the time the turkey was served, always by dessert. But after the dinner, as dusk gathered, all became quiet. The uncles left, my father went to sleep on the sofa, my mother went to her room, and my grandfather would take us children to the movies.

Almost all those people are gone now, but I see each one and the entire wild scene every time I sit down for Thanksgiving dinner, even way up here in Maine, and a thousand light years away from 65th Street.

The boats are surfacing from under the snow. Last October I brought them up from the bay—a seasonal ritual that had to be done for the first time without the help of the boys who were away at school, and will be away more and more as the Octobers pass. Each autumn the boats are laid in the same winter resting place, under the row of apple trees that runs across an edge of the meadow just in front of the house. There the boats lie, like beached whales, rolled over on their sides, and the snows of winter rise like the tide around them.

Each winter until this one I had been able to see the coppered boat bottoms bulging above the snow drifts—rust red fish surfacing in a vast white sea. But this winter the snow tide rose too high. My boats were buried. I almost forgot they were there until last week's rains washed away enough snow so the red hulls suddenly broke through and became a presence of the season, to be noted with every check of the landscape from the kitchen window. Now they are so much of a presence I know I shall have to attend to them before too long. For just as the ritual of autumn requires the boats to be beached, so does the ritual of spring demand that they be attended with paint, putty and preservatives.

It's an old story for me. I have almost always had boats. Like Toad in *Wind In The Willows,* I think there is nothing finer than puttering around with boats. And my boats have always been wooden, which means that no spring can pass without some attention being paid to the craft in question, otherwise, like a neglected woman, she will fail you when you most need her.

My first wooden boat was the *Emma*, named after my maternal grandmother; and in many ways I got to know the boat better than I ever knew the person. My brother and I (and this was more than twenty years ago) first discovered the *Emma*'s resilience when, as foolish, young teen-agers, we hauled the sixteen-foot, flat-bottomed, rowboat across the strand of beach that separated the boat's accustomed pond from a definitely unaccustomed Atlantic Ocean. We launched the *Emma* into the very, absolute, curling and pounding edge of the open Atlantic and rowed her through the feather-white surf as if she were a twenty-foot sea boat instead of a clumsy, narrow, square-sterned craft that had been purchased right off the floor at Macy's department store by my grandfather who had been raised on the streets of Brooklyn and had never been to sea in his life in anything smaller than an ocean liner.

We (my brother and I, and some not-so-fearless friends watching from the beach) pressed the *Emma* into this extraordinary service because we had discovered a sickly, but surprisingly large shark, cruising the edge of our beach. The big fish lolled like an invalid sunning himself in a deck chair, lying there in the wash of the waves that spent their fury breaking on the outer bar and then frothed across the flats onto the beach in a kind of sudsy foaming. The shark lay just inside the curl of the outer breakers, and that was where my brother and I rowed the *Emma*. As we got nearer the huge, triangular, dusky dorsal fin of the big fish, I stood up in the *Emma*'s pointy bow, trying to look as much like Captain Ahab as a skinny adolescent could. My brother, displaying more loyalty than sense, kept rowing and got us alongside the fish, which, as it turned out, was as long as the boat.

With the utter bravado of the young, I hurled an eel spear mounted on a broomstick into the broad back of the shark. There was one split second of petrified eternity as the fish felt the barbs break its skin and I and my brother knew we were in serious trouble. The shark rolled, turned its back and the eel spear against the side of the trembling *Emma*, snapped the broomstick, and then raised an ugly shark head from beneath the waves and took a bite of Macy's best that nearly ripped the entire length of *Emma*'s gunwale planking from bow to stern.

We were not so stupid that we hung around waiting for the

shark's next move, and we rowed the scarred boat to shore. I spent the next two weeks repairing *Emma's* battle damage and got my first taste of the charms of puttering around with wooden boats. I've been doing it ever since, which is why I was so pleased to see the dory and the pram surface at last from under the flood tide of this long winter's snows.

It's been a good summer. One of the best, when measured in the favorable setting for comparison that September gives us, with its soft mornings and tender dawns. There was no formal holiday for me, but the entire stretch of summer from June to Labor Day became a carnival of youth; and I suppose it was the youngness of the summer that made it good. The boys, especially Marsh, were with me in each of our romantic but clumsy efforts at clamming, eeling, fishing and fantasizing about the successes we could make. Because of the boys and the exciting integrity of their perception, the failures we did make seemed somehow incidental to the events that were shared.

The sharing with the young is over now. They have all moved their lives to the school routine. They are no longer omnipresent in my days; and because they have school, they are no longer to be dealt with as having days to give, but only evenings to use for the perfunctory exchange. So I am full of sadness about the death of this summer; through the young I was younger and back at the occupations of my youth.

I was thinking that the summer should not end as I drove Marsh and his school things along the exodus highway on the weekend. But wanting it not to end is far hotter than having it end with nothing more than a numb slide into the next season. Knowing how much I wanted it not to end made me certain of how good the summer had been.

There must have been another summer like it for me, because I recall the way I refused to allow its ending, and so ended it with a brutal finality that saved us both. Strangely, I have no memories of the summer itself, only of its epilogue.

The family had rented a summer house—an old farmhouse that had somehow managed to survive the pressures of a developing resort and had stayed genuine, near the center of town, as a cow might look today grazing on the Boston Common. I was a college freshman and left for my new educational career on the day the house was closed, the last rent paid and all of the family but myself returned to the city. I took the train to New Haven, with my college baggage and the key to a small shed on the edge of the lawn of our summer place.

The little locked building must have been a utility shed for the farmer who had built the place long before the town was overtaken by summer people. Between our family and previous tenants it had been converted to a kind of playhouse-clubhouse, depending on the age of the young who escaped to it from the big house across the lawn. It was, like all else at that place, well built, and it had a chimney, to which my brother and I had fixed an old wood-burning stove. We had also moved in a couple of beds and had managed to create a fine non-home for ourselves, just far enough away from home so we felt unoppressed.

Of course, it was no longer ours when the summer ended, but I took the key because I planned to come back, alone. Even New Haven, with its heady excitement, its rushing to get ready, did not dissuade me. I moved fast and cynically through registration, room-finding, etc. and on the day after I arrived I hitched the long awkward trip back to our summer place. It was the third week of September and the days ended in early evening. Dusk had come when I said good-bye to the last car and began to walk the last two miles to the little house.

It was not the same as it had been. The beds were stripped, the mattresses looked ugly, damp. Curtains were gone, and the starkness of the place almost overcame me with aloneness. But I was there; the summer had not ended. I kept thinking that as I walked to the village under elms shivering in the northwest wind and the growing coldness of a late September night. I ate in a small restaurant, was recognized, but not noticed. I went to a movie in the town's only theater, also strangely stark when stripped of its summer audience.

When I came out for the walk home the streets were empty; the wind had picked up and the cold had become a presence. The stars had their autumnal hardness in a clear dark sky, and I recall how the elm branches lashed back and forth in the wind, bending their black bows across the heavens. When I got to the shed, I built an awesome fire, but even it could not warm the place. The wind was too strong, too cold, too real, and what little sleep I got was between two raw mattresses I tried to use for warmth.

There was no water for washing when the bright sun came up with more wind the next morning, and I walked back to the village for a breakfast which I knew would be my last meal in that part of the world until the next summer. I had tried hard to keep mine from ending, and had arranged to evade all of man's obstacles. But I could not keep autumn from moving in; I could not, in the face of that cold and lonely wind, continue the self-deception I had so resolutely sought to maintain. My summer had ended that night.

Years later I learned that the village police had known of my visit. They had watched the little house, but whoever it was on night duty had said nothing. He knew, I think, how much some of us want some summers never to end.

The first "hot" day of the season has happened. I put "hot" in quotation marks because in Maine the term is strictly relative. Most people can live in Maine for years without learning what hot really means; some of them may never learn unless they leave the state. But it's "hot" for Maine today. When I walk in the sun, the slight exercise makes my shirt stick to my back and I can feel the sweat gathering on my brow. If I had to do any strenuous work, the sweat would run down into my eyes and my shirt would be soaked in a few minutes. For May, in Maine, that's hot.

The presence of heat, as an oppressive and palpable influence on life, never lasts long in Maine—even in mid-summer. By evening the listless air is moved by a sweet dark breeze blowing from the ocean all the way inland to places like Bangor and Veazie. As long as a man knows that night will bring surcease from heat, a day can be like an oven and be endured. In the cities, there is no such promise. There the concrete and asphalt store the day's heat and redistribute it through the night in even greater intensity and with even greater oppressiveness because the rocking heat comes long after the sun has set, and somehow that offends man's sensibilities.

That kind of city heat, that artificially created, man-constructed freak of nature, is the worst heat I can remember; but all of my worst memories are man-made. Nothing nature has done, even at the height of its violence, has ever approached man's work for its sheer unpleasantness. So there is not even a sentimental attachment to recalling other hot days on this first one of the warm months of 1969. I don't unfold the curled leaves of my memory hoping to find some pleasant tasting kernel of reminiscence about my time in the city; I know that each of those seeds will produce bitter fruit. So I avoid the city circuits of my mind and activate the ones that have to do with other hot days in the country, where it was the sun and the air alone that made the day bend under the sheer weight of its own heat.

Then I recall my first days in Burns, Oregon, and I know that I have established for all time the one memory landmark that will guide me back to my hottest day. This is a notable discovery, for from this time on in Maine or out, I will be able to ease whatever heat suffering is happening simply by dialing Burns, Oregon, on my mental computer and turning to thoughts of days when I was suffering more than I am now or in the future. For some asinine reason, the memory of worse suffering in the past always seems a remedy for present discomforts.

I was in Burns working for a lumber company during one of my college summers. Like many young men I was attracted by a job that would pay me for body-building in the sun and the wilds of the northwest woods. I had visions of myself returning in the fall a veritable Atlas, or Paul Bunyan, full of the mystique of the tall timber.

My job was to help the engineer who was "cruising timber" for the company. This meant he spent his days walking through the woods, checking the acres owned by the company, evaluating the number of board feet of lumber per acre, establishing the proper boundaries of the property and marking the route of logging roads that should be built when the cutting crews moved in.

My job consisted mostly of following the engineer and helping him look for corner markers, blazing trees and cutting center lines through the brush for the road routes he selected. It would have been a fine job, except that I had no idea how hot it could get in Burns, Ore. The first day the temperature was about 115° Farenheit on the obsidian flats we crossed between timber stands. We had already walked about five miles when we hit the flats, and that engineer walked as fast as most men jog.

Fresh from the classroom, I had long since finished my one canteen of water and my mouth was filled with a frightening natural phenomenon—the "cotton" that comes when the body's moisture is exhausted. The sun reverberated off the black rocks, my legs wobbled and I thought that if we ever got in the shade I would never leave again. Until then, I had had no idea that a person could actually be hurt so by sheer heat.

We did finally get to the woods and I fell flat on my belly beside a mud hole filled with the footprints and other leavings of stray beef cattle. But the depression held water covered with green scum that I brushed aside with my hand just before I put my entire face in the warm stuff and drank it as if it were the finest chilled champagne.

I have no other memories of heat's oppression that can surpass those of that one day. It's fine to think that now they help me stay cool.

Heroes in eighteenth-century novels (remember *Tom Jones*) were always running into people they had seen twenty years before; being saved by someone they had casually befriended as a child; discovering a note they had been carrying for a decade had become the clue to a treasure; and just generally making the most of incredible quirks of fate and random juxtapositions of people and events that threaded through the intricate design of their lives. I always believed that such bizarre patterns were only to be found in the pages of Dickens, Fielding, et al; but now that my life has run on long enough to encompass the kind of time fate needs to make itself known, I begin to wonder.

I wonder with renewed awe when I read news items like the one that appeared last week about the Ashland Oil Company's search for a refinery site in South Portland. According to one report which appeared in the *Portland Evening Express*, Ashland Oil wants 300 to 500 acres on Highland Avenue in South Portland for a refinery to process crude oil conveyed by pipeline from Portland Harbor.

The report appeared on the same day that *Maine Times* published an editorial of mine saying this newspaper had joined the ranks of those who believe it is in Maine's best interests to prohibit any and all expansion of any oil industry in the state. Coupled with the Ashland announcement, the juxtaposition of the editorial, my life, my present role in Maine and the arrival of Ashland as a leader of the oil offensive...well, it makes Dickens and Fielding seem quite real.

You see, I once worked for Ashland Oil. It was one of the few "companies" I ever worked for, and the only one remotely concerned with petroleum. It was in the autumn of 1948, the year I finally graduated from Yale. After my final exams (I wouldn't go to graduation) I got a dandy summer job as the skipper of the Fishers Island Country Club launch. Fishers Island is a few miles off New London (Conn.) at the gateway to Long Island Sound. Lots of wonderfully wealthy people spend their summers on Fishers. The clubhouse (since torn down) looked like something out of The Great Gatsby, and in that setting I behaved rather like a Fitzgerald character, surrounded by beautiful people, a beautiful place, and enjoying a spectacular success as the club's only boat captain. It was the first time the club had provided a launch service for its members, and the experimental financial arrangements were grossly overbalanced in my favor. I made a fantastic amount of money and totally exhausted even my youthful self trying to debauch long enough and expensively enough to spend all I was making. I almost killed myself, and my friends, but could not avoid finishing the summer with some money in the bank.

I returned to the family in New York City and proceeded to live in indolence long enough to continue my spending crusade. The spectacle just about drove my father out of his mind. He was enraged that a college graduate should begin his career running a fishing boat; but totally apoplectic that I had made such a financial success of it. When I had finally exhausted myself and my funds, my father made his move. He asked me what my plans were; of course, I had none, except rest. He then bludgeoned me with the spectacle of unemployment, told me he had gone to great (and final) efforts to get me a job, explained that there was much money (I didn't want it, at that point) to be made in the oil business, and said that the president of Ashland Oil was a friend of his who would keep an eye on me.

Two days later I was on the train for Ashland, Kentucky, the home office and refinery of Ashland Oil. It is also (or was) the site of a large steel mill, and the huge, grey slag heap was the first thing I saw when I got off the train. It was a long, long way from the sparkling waters of Fishers Island.

So was my job. Instead of rising with the sun to hunt for bluefish in the bright briny off Race Rock, I got up in the dark to work the night shift as a quality-control tester in the Ashland Oil Refinery laboratory. I checked samples of kerosene and other petroleum products for color, purity, factors and flash points, all of which I dutifully recorded on a sheet for the day shift. Considering I was the only student to get an X in my analytical chemistry class at Yale (I dropped my test sample in the sink), I thought I did quite well not to cause a disaster at Ashland.

But my life there was a lonely disaster. I was not cut out for business, oil, or living alone in a dreary Kentucky mill town when all my beautiful people were back on the coast. Yet I could not face my father after quitting the job he got for me in a place where the president was watching me. So I went from Ashland to St. Louis to work for the Post Dispatch. (Old Joe Pulitzer was one of the beautiful people I had taken bluefishing.) About three days after I arrived in St. Louis, the newspapers went on strike and I ended up wrapping china Christmas gifts in a cubbyhole at Scruggs, Vandervoort and Barney—the local Jordan Marsh.

I came back to New York in the spring with my own job as a copy writer, and my father and I were in a state of fragile co-existence; our war was over. Hostilities continued to subside as I made a rather fantastic and flamboyant New York career for myself as

121

a public relations man. After a year or so of this, my father and I could talk once again as human beings, and one day at lunch at his club he told me a funny story. "You know," he said, smiling, "I saw the president of Ashland Oil about two weeks ago. He asked me how you are coming along at his Kentucky plant." Then my father laughed, a rare thing for him. "Boy," he said, his eyes watering and his big frame shaking, "He's really keeping an eye on you, isn't he?"

In case the president thinks I'm still working for Ashland, he will realize his oversight if his company comes to Maine. But this time he really will keep his eye on me, just as my father said he would twenty years ago.

It was (to continue last week's thoughts) the northwest wind which eventually blew me from the city where I was born, raised, lived and worked for some thirty years. I do not think of this as an odd way of explaining my departure from an urban career and life style. There are, I am convinced, ageless chords deep within men that can still be strummed by the simplest of natural events. Man lived with, within and against nature for too many centuries to now be able to abandon all natural ties, as if his heritage were a disposable wrapper he could shuck without thought or consequence.

In that September of my exodus, the northwest wind brought its promise of bright skies, its cotton clouds, its high barometers and stirred the same migratory urges in me that it stirs every September in falcons, bluefish and sea scoters. All men must feel some of those same stirrings on these first golden September days although they may not acknowledge them. The ties are too elemental to have been crushed even by today's technological monsters. Men respond to the first autumnal northwesters; the wind does more than bend the grass or toss the trees. It stirs the soul and breathes a fresh and sudden vitality into the body. It is the elemental force that can start a man on a new adventure—the fairest of winds for sailing uncharted shores.

122

There were few landmarks for me when I left the city and became a working fisherman. But there were the bright September days, the northwest winds and the same ocean landscape I had wanted ever since I had been a boy. After twenty years, I had come back, moved by some inner force to do whatever had to be done to stay close to the shore and sea, away from the city grit.

There was nothing easy in the change. The warm September became October, then November clamped the beach in the chill of its eternal gray. The northwest winds were no longer gentle; they were sharpened to a keen cold edge on winter's harsh stone, and they blew too long. The winds were beyond me and all men; I could not shape them to my romantic whims, anymore than I could make the ocean calm whenever I set sail upon it.

But the first winter ice did not defeat me. I stayed, and spring and summer came. By the following September I was no longer thinking of becoming a fisherman; I was one, and I was out under the wings of the northwest wind every day, all day, and it was then that I became aware of the total vitality of the wind's migratory force.

I was bluefishing that first full fall, with my friend Jim. We hand-lined from his boat; which is to say we trolled as many as eight lengths of tarred line, sweeping like long tailfeathers off the boat's wide stern and spreading bamboo outriggers. At one end of the line, feathered lures concealed sharp hooks; at the boat end, the lines were cushioned by strips of rubber inner tube, built into the rig to stretch and absorb the first jolting punch of a striking fish.

Those bluefish off Montauk were heavyweights—10, 12, 14-pounders. Wild and tearing, electrified by the northwest wind, their thrashing schools gathered off the point for a feeding frenzy, a kind of final meal before the migratory journey. None of us knew where the bluefish came from, or where they went on their compulsive travels so hidden by the silent sea. We knew only that they most often surfaced with the first nor'westers, and that when they did, the excitement of their presence was almost unbearable.

As the sun moved to the west, the wings of white terns became pink in the soft rays. Screaming at a relentless and frantic pitch, the tiny sea birds hovered in swirling flocks over the feeding fish, diving and darting into the bloody confusion for whatever scraps surfaced from the bluefish feast. Oil and blood spreading from lacerated herring and other prey slicked the wind ruffled water; big fish broke the surface in great gouts of white water, and, as I tended the lines, Jim would shout and steer the boat toward these foamy signals raised by the fish themselves. Often three or four lines would stretch at the same moment as the lures were hit by the fish. With wet, water-wrinkled hands, I hauled the surging fish to the boat, unhooked them, and tossed the lure back—if all went well. Often the fish broke loose, mangled the lure, parted the line, or dropped free just as I tried to swing it over the gunwale.

On the good days, we headed for port after sundown with 300 or 400 pounds. We had been up since dawn, the fish still had to be gutted, washed, weighed and iced; the boat had to be washed down, refueled and secured for the night. We hadn't eaten much but crackers and apples since dawn, and we had to be back before the sun came up. But, blowing from somewhere thousands of years away in time, that northwest wind brought me the energy and exuberance to think of the entire experience as a voyage of sheer joy.

Jim kept on fishing. I left him after seven years for full-time newspapering. I don't know if I could last a complete bluefish day; I do know I wouldn't try it without the help of the northwest wind.

Freed from their classrooms like puppies turned out of their pen, the children went scampering to the beach last week for the first time this year. When I got home in the early evening of that warm day, the beach people had just returned and their wet towels, plastic jugs that had been full of ice and sugar drinks, wet bathing suits, beach balls and surfing mattresses—all their paraphernalia lay scattered on the lawn, and over the entire confusion was the fine white sand and the fragrance of salt water that will be with us now until late in September.

Of the many blessings of life in this corner of the world, I find none more blessed than the beach and there is a fine and honest continuity in seeing the children's summer lives involved with the surf and the sand and the sea. For I think the beaches of the northeast Atlantic are the finest in the world, and the few beaches in Maine are becoming the best of these.

There is no mystery about my love for beaches. In the first year of my life my summer was spent in a rambling house, perched like some huge and clumsy sea bird on a high dune peering out over an Atlantic Ocean that stretched across the world. The house was so close to the sea that my small bed trembled as each wave broke; and on stormy days the foamy fringes of the surf curled along the edge of the terrace.

I spent many summers in that place. When I was five or six I was taught to swim in the surf and I can still feel the awe and excitement of diving into the elemental curl of a breaking wave and letting it enfold me in its dark and fluid turbulence. Later, in my young teens, the other boys of that beach and myself would spend entire day after entire day body surfing the waves, no matter how rough the waters or cold the sky.

And still later, I spent years on the very same beach, long after the sea-bird house had changed hands. I fished from the beach in a net-heavy dory that pushed through the waves breaking on the same spot where I had learned to swim.

So in my life, finding a beach was like going home, and I looked for beaches everywhere I went—the mine-strewn beaches of England; the rocky coasts of France and Italy with their limp, warm seas; the tropical waters of Florida with the barracuda and Portuguese men-of-war; the waters off Savannah, muddied by the southern red clay brought down by the rivers of the south; the long reaches off the Carolinas; the sharky beaches of South America and the mini-beaches of the Carribean; the cold, kelpy beaches of the Pacific in northern California; the muggy beaches off New Orleans on the hot Gulf; and the spongy, coral beaches of Bermuda—I looked for beaches everywhere I went and with all the objectivity I can muster I still argue that the beaches of the northeast Atlantic are the finest in the world.

The proper combination of wind and water temperature makes the Atlantic here the most invigorating and refreshing of all bathing seas. Perhaps it is the combining of the Gulf Stream fringe with the North Atlantic current, or some much more mysterious ecological recipe; but whatever it is, there is no water like the waters off these shores. Nor are there other beaches more pure, more free of annoyances like the sharp coral of warmer seas, the stinging leftovers of the men of war, the smell of sharks, the rocky shores, the flies and insects — none of these is here in any noticeable presence, yet one or more of them is part of every other beach place.

I began to realize the exceptional quality of these beaches during the travels that took me to beaches in other places, but not until I spent a year in Ohio did I know the lancing pangs of being without any beach. I felt as if some of the fabric of my life had been ripped from me and buried. I could not breathe free, and the midwestern air without a beach to blow from became a suffocation.

I spent most of the year planning ways to leave, and it was my determination to escape that brought me to Maine. I remember my first hours in Kennebunk on a raw March day as I was driven on a tour of the town. We came around a point at Kennebunk Beach and there was my ocean, the great spring swells of an equinoctial storm curling and crashing on that lovely stretch of sand. I can still see them, still feel the surge inside me that told me I could never again deny a nearness to the sea.

I don't expect the children to necessarily share my need, but it is right and fitting that they should know these beaches. There is no other place in the world where they can run as free; and there are no longer any beaches left as free as ours in Maine.

"The Jogger," as the children have named him, still jogs by the house every day, rain, sun, sleet or snow. He leaves his car parked down the road and runs around the four-road, five-mile circuit that winds through the woods and meadows here where we live. He has been trotting by for two years now, and when we see him we wave, and he waves back and smiles. He is quite discreet about his exercise and never stops to puff with health, shaming me into looking down at my slouching waist line.

I appreciate the consideration, and think of The Jogger (it will be something like being told there is no Santa Claus if I ever learn his real name) with kind thoughts. I have tried his kind of conditioning, and found it wanting. One raw November afternoon, I allowed the national jogging fad to catch me off guard and ended up trying to trot from the house to the landing. It's less than a half-mile down there and back, but I had to quit jogging even before I got to the bay. It seemed a boring pastime to me—too violent to allow me to absorb the countryside, and too demanding of my unconditioned physique to give me anything but short breath and a sense of helpless anger at being so exposed as a middle-aged wheezer.

But I have never been quite the same since, because as I listened to the rasping of the air scraping in and out of my flabby lungs, I realized that I was, indeed, out of shape. A cruel person might have called me a physical wreck, but I stayed in hiding until I got my wind back and was able to meet my public with composure. As I went to bed that night I thought I would begin some sort of regimented exercise the very next day. But in the few minutes of thought I gave the matter before I went to sleep, I was unable to come up with a method for making conditioning a pleasure. After all, the military had ruined calisthenics for me, lifting weights is done seriously for competition only, and I had no time for tennis, golf, squash or any of those other sports that successful businessmen always seem to have time for.

But that was in November. I think now that I have found the answer, and I hope to start a Maine conditioning fad, if not a national one. My exercise is rowing. The only drawback, compared with jogging, is the economics of the situation. These days it costs something close to $50 and a little work to put together a rowboat that will stay afloat long enough to allow you to stop bailing long enough to get in some serious rowing. Of course that's a lot less than it takes to play golf, or tennis, or lift weights, but not quite as Scotch as jogging, which needs nothing except a pair of sneakers.

If you compare rowing and jogging, however, you'll find rowing well worth the small difference in price. The key to the entire concept is in the proposition that physical fitness need not be painful; or, to state it another way, with rowing, one cannot only live longer, but enjoy doing it.

The thing about rowing is that it doesn't let you know that you're exercising. When I run down the road for more than a few steps, I begin puffing and I say to myself it's good that you've got that pain in your side, because it means some tattered muscle is being re-knit. But I really don't believe what I'm telling myself and I know only that it's good that I'm in pain because that is the Puritan ethic, and I have never shaken my Calvinist ties. I have enough sympathy with the hedonists, however, to know that if I find something that gives me pleasure and also keeps me in shape, I've made one of life's major discoveries.

That's how I feel about rowing. Every muscle moves when I row; stomach, legs, thighs, arms, wrists and hands, all of them feel the pull as I put my back into stroking the oars and making the old dory push through the wavelets. I'm exercising; I'm straining; I'm really getting in shape; but I'm also reveling in nostalgia, taking off on a voyage of important discovery and getting myself as far away from telephones as possible. It is a miracle that any man could be improving his condition by indulging in all these delights. Even my Calvinist conscience is satisfied with the deal, because when the rowing day is over, I can feel the lilting aches here and there and I know I have suffered enough to be improved, even though I never felt a thing but bliss while I was rowing.

Also, rowing kindles my dreams and fires my memories. I have been rowing, I would guess, since before I was ten. The skill came to its ultimate test when I fished for bass and had to row a net heavy dory through the open surf. It was totally glorious, and I re-live it all every time I go down to the bay with my oars. Then I come back and wave to The Jogger in peace.

In keeping with its often warped sense of values, the public paid little more than routine attention last week to the destruction of a ship and the loss of its entire crew. In a mortal struggle just a short distance off the coast of Maine, the tanker *Keo* was torn asunder by an Atlantic storm, and its crew swept into the sea from the aft section of the vessel to which they clung through the dark and wild hours of Wednesday night. This happened in spite of combined rescue efforts by the U.S. Coast Guard, the Air Force, and private vessels in the *Keo's* vicinity.

I do not complain about the callous public which pays more attention to the novel and bizarre than it does to the grim and the tragic; nor do I suggest that today's technology should be able to save the lives of thirty-six at sea just as well as it protects the lives of two on the moon. These are rather obvious observations, and while they may be relevant, they are recorded in every tragedy comparable to the *Keo's*. Scores of Gloucester fishermen die at sea every year, and their violent passing goes almost unrecorded and unnoticed.

What I think should be considered more seriously is the monumental reality of the sea's power—an elemental, environmental force which has taken so many lives over the years that thirty-six more drownings are not really news. I think that if the message of the sea is understood, perhaps some people who have developed a dangerous disregard of natural forces may be persuaded to re-evaluate their position. Or, to state it another way, if people could comprehend the *Keo* sinking, they might realize that nature is not to be tampered with unless men are fully prepared for the consequences.

Few men who have spent any time at sea, for example, would countenance the dispersal of chemical poisons over the landscape. For a man who has been aboard ship in a storm has been converted by sheer power to an understanding of man's relationship to nature. He comes to understand, often from an experience as simple as looking a thirty-foot wave in the face, that the natural events which sustain life on this planet are events which move inexorably through a cycle. If that cycle is disturbed, if man sets himself against nature, then it is man, not nature, who courts disaster.

Disaster, of course, is not inevitable. But some kind of struggle is unavoidable. The message of the *Keo* is that the struggle must be anticipated as must the ruthlessness with which nature plays its adversary role. Those who do not grasp the reality of nature's ruthless qualities are those who lose the struggle. In their ignorance, they are fearless, reckless, greedy, or just plain stupid.

I was both stupid and reckless when I first went to sea, and the sea was quick to discover my faults and to teach me the grave liabilities of my ignorance. Those lessons are an experience I have never forgotten.

There were times in the beginning of my days on the water when the lessons were put to me more gently; but I was too occupied with my own self-esteem to take notice. It required real terror before I came to my senses and realized the inexorable price the sea exacts from those who treat it too lightly.

The day was not a special day; the boat was a small double-ended fishing boat crafted by fine fishermen on the Gaspe Peninsula. It was their knowledge of the sea built into that boat that saved me, not my seafaring skill, which reduced itself to clutching the tiller and praying. I was moving the boat from one harbor to another, and my journey took me only about twenty miles. But during that trip, the wind began to blow much harder than I had thought possible, and it came from a quarter which left me no protection. Pushing steadily off the open sea, the gale piled up larger and larger waves—short, punching seas that became even sharper when the tide changed and the current began to move against the wind.

The boat was getting pushed around. I could not hold my course, the pump was running steadily to keep the bilges emptied of the seas that were breaking green over the bow. I was making little progress, dusk would catch me before I reached my harbor, and in the growing darkness and my gathering fear, I began cursing the sea for its unrelenting punishment. Alone on the boat, seeing for the first time how little was the margin of safety left to me by the wind and waves, I realized the damn sea could sink me, and no one would ever know why I had been out there. But the sea did not respond to my curses or my fear. It simply kept coming on with bigger waves, more water over my bow, more spray in my face, and the awful realization that if some change weren't made, my engine would quit and I'd be adrift.

All I could do was hold on, pray that wind and the seas would stop their pummeling. As the sun went down, the wind did subside, and I got to safe harbor—late, wet and scared. The end of that trip marked the end of my days as a reckless sailor. I went to sea thousands of times afterwards, but never without knowledge of the consequences. The sea became a presence, instead of surface. And that presence, in turn, became part of the larger presence that is the reality of our environment. By not paying attention to the *Keo*, much of the public may be missing a lesson the sea is trying to teach. Missing too many can only mean danger for mankind.

Lawrence Durrell, the author of Justine, Clea, Mountolive, and other opulent stories of the Mid East, says in one of his books that each of us has a landscape in our memories which is our "home landscape" — a place held forever in the circuits of our mind's eye to which we return throughout our lives, in dreams, in reminiscence, and in the fleeting images of the past we use to evaluate the present.

I learned of the Durrell premise about two months ago, and ever since have been trying to establish my home landscape. For although I believe in the concept, I have found it difficult to be honest enough with myself to make the final determination. A soul who has forever lived with the same landscape — and there must be many such souls in Maine — has, of course, no problem. There is just one landscape for him; it is his life and his home. For a person like me, however, whose life has been spaced with amazing regularity in five-year periods of location and occupation, determining the home landscape is more difficult.

It presents, among other things, problems of self-analysis that had perhaps better be left alone. My love for Maine, for example, might appear a bit flighty to Maine if I confessed that my home landscape seems to be in another state. I mean, after all, when Maine and I have such a stable relationship underway, why upset it with the news that a former love still lives in my memory.

Or shall I say to Maine that she will be my home landscape when the time of my life has run on long enough here in this one place, for this is the place I have decided to stay. I must say something like that to ease the blow, because if I have a home landscape now, it is the eastern end of Long Island (N.Y.) where I spent no more time than I have elsewhere, but where I must have endured enough emotional heat and stress to weld the look of the place forever in my memory. If my mind flashes into the past, it is always into the landscape of those long stretches of beach, the open, harsh Atlantic, the reaches of salt marsh, the soft risings of the sand dunes or the fertile waters of tidal ponds. Much of it exists no longer, which is why I am in Maine, but when my minds eye sees into the vortex of my past, it sees me on that flat, windswept, bright and salty land.

I will give you an example, and then you can test yourself to see where your home landscape lies. When the dry air arrived last week and pushed the soggy days to sea, there came also that crystalline clarity that belongs more to September than to August. And on certain rare days, the wind stops, but the clarity stays, as if the day is caught in amber. When you look across the bay, the water's surface stretches like a silken banner, colored with the blue of sky and stretched taut from shore to shore.

When I saw our part of Casco Bay stretched tight in the stillness, the instant recall of my mind had me "picking up" bay scallops at Three Mile Harbor — and I knew my home landscape had pulled at me again.

Bay scallops are not to be found in Maine, except as ecological rarities. Their larger brothers are here, however, and there are enough similarities between the two relatives so sea scallopers will know what I'm talking about. Those of you who know neither sea or bay scallop are missing so much I scarcely know where to start. You'll have to settle for the information that the bay scallop is a small bivalve (shellfish) shaped like the Shell Oil symbol, only this one has a thin shell about three inches across which shields a morsel of meat so tasty it defies description.

On the September amber days at Three Mile, I used to drift in a boat moved only by the silent currents of the tide. Perched on the gunwale with my face pressed almost to the surface of the windless water, I watched for scallops on the bottom five or six feet down and tried to flip them into my long-handled net with its tiny, sock-like bag. The sun beat on my back, the air hung still and the bay's fantastic bottom moved under me like the surface of a strange planet. Scallops did their crazy gyrations as they escaped my net; or those that didn't piled up on deck where they snapped and clicked their shells.

I can still see it all, even though I perhaps had only five good pick-up days in five years. That's why I know the truth about my home landscape; but I don't quite know how to explain it to Maine. She isn't wearing Casco Bay just to make me remember another love.

MORE ABOUT MAINE

There has been a great deal written recently in national publications about the approaching cultural crisis of our times. No one is quite sure of the causes, but many have done a good job of describing the effects. These include the incredible increase in crimes of personal violence in the nation's cities; the general personal rudeness and hostility which makes city store clerks snarl and restaurant waiters openly insulting; the tendency of city dwellers to withdraw from the human race to the point where they refuse to pick up the telephone and call police while a girl is being murdered within sight and sound; the growing incidence of looting, shoplifting, stealing and other forms of showing total disregard for property rights; the continuing trend toward the glamorization of criminals; the callousness with which the quality of life in cities is destroyed by air, water and street pollution from corporations and citizens alike; the growing hostility of teachers to students and vice-versa; and the general breakdown of the unwritten laws of any urban society.

Among the several theories which explain this social phenomenon are the arguments: (1) change is occuring so fast that urban man cannot adjust, grows increasingly anxious and therefore increasingly violent; (2) too many people are crowded into too little space in cities, resulting in the breakdown of "normal" behavior patterns; (3) damage to the entire urban environment is so great that people fight with each other because they are unable to locate and fight with the invisible bureaucracy that has ruined their life styles.

I am giving you back what I read more and more frequently, and what I see with increasing repetition on my less and less frequent visits to cities. One result of all this is an admittedly smug reassurance that Maine is a great place to live because here people still treat each other like human beings. Another result is a kind of guilt about enjoying Maine life so much while those who are not here are faced with such daily violence and desperation. And finally, I wonder often what can be done to preserve what is best about Maine living, while, at the same time, hopefully making it strong enough to be exported to the beleaguered cities.

All of which leads me to one small suggestion. I began thinking about it when I first went "way down east" about a year ago. I was traveling mostly to Machias (reporting the first of many chapters in the oil story) but made side trips to several small coastal communities which I knew I would never see unless I made the effort while I was in the region.

I was driving down the road to Starboard Village on the Machiasport peninsula when an elderly fellow walking along the roadside waved to me as I passed. The greeting caught me off guard, and I did not wave back. I thought perhaps the man had mistaken my car for one that he may have known that normally traveled the road.

After three days in the area, I realized the wave was no mistake. People walking in that part of the country wave to everyone who drives by, whether or not they know them. The wave is a simple, direct, artless and genuine greeting; a salutation that silently says "Welcome, fellow man, whoever you are". Towards the end of my stay, I acknowledged all waves with a wave of my own, and I felt great doing it.

But I stopped when I left that region. As I got back to the more traveled section of the southern coast where I lived, I stopped waving because I thought people would think me a fool—some sydcophant trying for attention.

Then later this year I motored far into Maine again, this time in the lumber towns and hamlets around Millinocket; and no sooner had I gotten there and was heading through the dusk to my assignment but I passed a man walking along the road. He was dressed in a red wool shirt, wore lumberman's boots and, as I passed, he waved. As soon as I saw the hand go up, I raised mine and I felt a tremendous gratitude at finding yet another Maine place so far from turmoil that strangers could start out with at least a visible signal of mutual acknowledgement.

I got more waves during my time there. They stopped when I left the byways for the turnpike, but this time I didn't. I waved at people I passed in other cars, and pedestrians I passed along the roadside. Perhaps it was a kind of silly thing to do. I got very few waves in return, and many puzzled looks, asking in essence: Now why should that fellow wave? I don't know him.

The looks weren't enough to make me stop waving, and I'm still at it. I don't keep my hand going all the time, but when I drive past people who are walking and who look at me and the car, I wave. I hope that after they get over their quizzicalness about whether they know me, the people may realize my gesture was nothing more than a greeting—the same kind of greeting given everyone by those serene folks way down east and way back in the timber. And I also hope, of course, that some of you will begin to revive the custom in all the rest of Maine. It's a small thing, a wave, but big enough if it reminds you that the fellow you wave at is your brother.

If there are special qualities which set Maine folk apart from those in other places, then good manners is certainly one of them. I don't mean the sort of "manners" practiced by courtiers and diplomats as a screen for often uncivilized acts; I mean manners which are good because they are sincere and because they spring from a genuine consideration for another person's feelings. That's the kind of good manners Maine people have, and they have put me to shame on many occasions.

I find good manners here everywhere I go. Even the busiest Maine people seem able to take the time to be courteous and considerate. At post offices, banks, super markets, restaurants, shops and stores, the clerks, waitresses, counter and check-out people always seem to find time to say a gentle word. Impatience, irritation and curtness jump out once in a while; but so rarely that all they do is remind me that Maine folk are also only human.

Perhaps I notice the good manners of people in public places because it is such a contrast to the attitudes of city people in the same places. Living the first 30 years of my life with New York City as headquarters left me expecting nothing from clerks except some service, and most of the time I felt lucky to get that.

But the attitudes of the people who serve the public are not the only yardstick by which I measure Maine's good manners. I am always warmed by the gentle environment of Maine's shops and stores; but I know that the gentleness might evaporate if the public became as pressing as it is in so many cities.

Yet, if that public stays a Maine public, it may never press too hard. The real test of considerateness comes when you must meet and communicate with people who have good reason to be wary and cool. Because of the nature of myself and my profession, I have been in many Maine situations in which I would have forgiven others for not being helpful or pleasant. They had every reason not to be; they knew in advance that my editorials or my articles were in disagreement with their views on the same issue. In many cases, I've had to call on department heads of the very departments I criticize yet in almost every case, those department heads displayed such beautiful Maine manners that I never cease to be re-impressed.

Those manners are characterized by an essential gentleness, an honesty, a caring for the preservation of a person's dignity, while at the same time he is allowed his independence. Maine manners are at once a tolerance and a grace. They are beautiful, and a wonder to behold.

I am especially aware of them now because I have seen them on display at two recent public meetings attended by an honest cross-section of Maine. Both meetings were on the subject of the proposed oil refinery for Sears Island. One, in Camden, was attended by about 400 persons, of whom some 395 were opposed to the idea of oil in their Penobscot Bay. The man they were listening to, James Keefe, commissioner of the Department of Economic Development, said he was in favor of the refinery and would not alter his position no matter what bay area residents (like those in the audience) said or did. Given that sort of confrontation, manners might have been expected to go by the boards. But (with one exception) that did not happen. Instead, just the opposite took place. Every question, every comment made from the floor to Mr. Keefe was phrased in soft language, asked in a gentle voice and delivered with great patience and consideration for Mr. Keefe's humanity. It was a lovely performance; a fine example of what the world could be if only the gentleness of Maine could somehow be exported.

(It was my own outburst of temper which was the one exception; it was a loud example of bad manners, yet the people there tolerated it with the same grace that they listened to Commissioner Keefe. In doing so, they taught me yet another lesson.)

The second meeting was at Searsport, and given the pre-meeting confusion and tension, almost any scene could have been excused,,,and I for one was prepared for any scene. I should have known better. Once again the manners of those Maine people were so full of tolerance that they put tension out of the hall. The event was a delight to witness, a kind of reassurance that with such manners, the world could be made infinitely better.

I worry, though, if Maine's good manners will not be erased by the pressures of a world which has all but forgotten the importance of consideration. I pray this does not happen; it would be so much better if the scales tipped the other way and Maine's beautiful manners could spread beyond these borders like a gentle breeze sent to dispel the graceless inhumanity of so many other men.

Those of us who live on the coast—where the sea's perpetual wildness dominates the land—tend too often to think of inland Maine as a far off place, inhabited by a different people as well as a different landscape. There are differences, yes; but the place is still Maine, and each time I wander through the Maine midlands I realize anew how smug us coastal folk can get if we allow that smugness to hold us on the edge of the sea.

I went down new roads in the midlands last week, roads I had never traveled before, and I came away with thoughts that have carried well to the sea, and stay with me beyond a tide or two. Moving over the small midland roads is a time trip more than a space jaunt. In July's mid-summer pause when the sun seems to stop, caught at the sky's peak and held there to shed its heat on the droning countryside, the trees over the midland roads become the arches of dark, cool tunnels. I travel through the deep green tunnels, grateful for their shade and bemused by the flashing patterns of light and shadow made by limbs, leaves and sky. There is so much land, I think, knowing that there are few places in the world a person can travel for so long under such unbroken green timbered canopies.

Every now and then a house goes by. There is a bit of a warning of its presence in the first fence post, or rock wall corner. But these don't come quite soon enough to allow me to slow to study the house; it flashes past, usually white clapboard, with a barn that has a sagging door fronting on a patch of worn bare ground where generations of horses and wagons and tractors have turned; and where now that the farm has died, a car turns to take its owner to work each morning, or to market each day.

What do these folks do, I wonder; how do they live so far out in the country. They must love it, to be so remote, to have to drive so far. Their solitary houses are inland islands, scattered far apart on this green, timbered sea, each barn a mooring which holds every old farm to its ground. Three or four generations ago, these Maine farms were the strength of the state. Now only a few are worked, but the others go on giving. They give solitude and the spirit of the land to the folks who would be crushed by the concrete of cities.

Then the house and barn are gone; the stone wall disappears into the woods and I am tunnel traveling again. It is so unlike my Maine, this dark and somnolent summer country. There are no other people on the road, even though it's a busy time of day, and I think perhaps they are all at their noon dinners, sitting at the big farm tables, parched hands scratchy from haying since dawn, drinking switchel and lemonade, eating meat pies, buttermilk biscuits and the other farm working food I have read about. But I know they are not; they are gone somewhere, these people— to Augusta, or Lewiston, or Waterville, where they make their day's pay so they can return to the farms at evening, like the sailor come back to his ship.

Often there are lakes at the ends of the green tunnels. The trees fall away and there is sudden blue beside the car. Come upon suddenly like this, the lakes of Maine are spectacular and shattering. The chrome green of the marsh grass pushes hard at the ultramarine blue; it is an incredible juxtaposition of brilliance in the fiery July sun. I see it and in the shimmering split second I understand what it is that brings the city refugees to these lakes. Even as I move by, I can see the trailers, the camper-trailers, the A-frames, the cottages, the tents, the camps, the aluminum boats, the six-packs, the wet bathing suits, the fishing rods, the 55-horse outboards, the sneakers, the potato salads, the tanned children and the sunburned fathers. They come and cluster around Maine's summer lakes pushing for space at the rim of the waterhole so they can swallow enough of a vacation to last them for eleven months of drought on a city block, or parched living in a surburban city.

Beyond one lake there is the vast openness of huge cleared fields—what must have been a truly important farm, more like the West than Maine, with its barbed wire fences. But Maine is there in the fields, caught in the granite boulders bulging from the hard ground, unyielding rock islands washed by a sea of ripening meadow grass. The aroma of the browning grass comes through my open window, and in it there is the summer's end, the fragrance of fall. I see the broken, gray and sagging wagon, dying alone in the deserted field; I sense the end of one more summer, gone like each of the bittersweet others. I hurry to get home.